The Ten Minute Strategist

Martin Turner

inGenios

Published by Ingenios Books
Fabrieksstraat 63, 9030 Zaventem, Belgium

The 10 Minute Strategist
© Martin Turner 2018
All rights reserved
21 20 19 18   4 3 2 1
First Edition

Every reasonable attempt has been made to identify
owners of copyright. Errors or omissions will be corrected
in subsequent editions.

ISBN: 9781980750956

Contents

Just ten minutes

Napoleon Bonaparte valued generals who could take in the strategic aspects of the terrain at a single glance. Alexander the Great created new tactics on the battlefield. The history of successful strategy is a history of people who thought fast. Which is completely the opposite of how most modern organisations do strategy. Organisational strategy today is like elephants wading through treacle: cumbersome, and somewhat comic, unless you happen to be the elephant.

This book is not about ten minute strategy, but about the ten minute strategist: an important distinction. Most strategies will fail. One estimate[1] suggests 90% will. But the ones which succeed are not those produced with the largest number of consultants, or the most intricate PowerPoint slides. They are produced by people who have practised strategy until it becomes second-nature: people who can put together—on their own and in a few minutes—something that will outperform the

1 I suspect it was an estimate made to make a point, rather than based on comprehensive analysis, but the figure tallies with my own experience.

90%, no matter how many elephants were engaged to tread the treacle.

Strategies fail for four fundamental reasons. Some are overwhelmed by circumstances. To some extent, that is unavoidable. For every strategy, there is at least one possible combination of events which will kill it. But that isn't the biggest reason.

Some strategies succumb to internal resistance. That can be hard to manage, though a good strategy should be able to anticipate it. Others are doomed by their own contradictions and inconsistencies: there are far more truly terrible strategies out there than good ones. By far the biggest reason for strategic failure, though, is that organisations never get round to implementing them. For most, strategy formation is a huge and cumbersome beast. Strategies take months or years to create. It takes armies of analysts. The strategic plan is hundreds of pages long. By the time the strategy has been constructed, the situation on which it was based has fundamentally changed. So the strategy gets put in a drawer, and the organisation reverts to doing the same old same old thing it always does.

Most organisations that have some awareness of their history of strategic failures respond by doing exactly what they shouldn't do. They hire more consultants, plan longer lead times, invest more in analysis, construct more elaborate hierarchies and print longer documents. It becomes increasingly difficult for even senior management to remember what the strategy is about, or why it was necessary. Those tasked with executing it have next to no chance. And so it goes.

From time to time, especially in a crisis, people step up who have an uncanny knack of rapidly getting to the heart of the problem, producing an actionable plan, and executing it, all in less time than it takes others to grasp the situation.

These are the ten minute strategists, the 'lucky' generals who somehow always seem to get the breaks.[2]

Is this through superior intelligence, better schooling, a strategic sixth sense, or some kind of luck, fate or destiny? Experience in other fields suggests that, whatever our natural advantages, the thing which makes the biggest difference is simply practice.

Not all strategies can be done in ten minutes. As a rule of thumb, allow for strategy making 1/10th to 1/20th of the amount of time it will take for execution. For a five year plan, you can afford three to six months. If you spent that long on a one year plan, there would be little time left for execution.

In a crisis, ten minutes may be all you get. But ten minutes is enough to step back, strategise, and come up with an approach which is better than the obvious 'bulldozer' approach, and also better than the protocol or residual approach that you, your friends, or your organisation adopt by force of habit.

This book is inspired by the ten schools of strategy identified by Mintzberg, Ahlstrand and Lampel in their seminal 'Strategy Safari'[3], although we will often take their structure in a different direction. Strategy Safari's Ten Schools are:

- Environmental
- Cognitive
- Entrepreneurial
- Political
- Positioning
- Cultural
- Planning
- Learning
- Design
- Transformation/Configuration

2 The idea of 'lucky generals' is usually attributed to Napoleon, but it was actually Cardinal Mazarin who said it.

3 Strategy Safari, Mintzberg, Ahlstrand and Lampel, FT Prentice Hall

How many strategies do people create in their entire lives? In most of the organisations I've worked for, some kind of long-term strategic plan was put together once every three to five years, and refreshed annually. But only the directors got to do the strategy bit.

To be a director in most organisations, you need to be at least forty, and more likely fifty or sixty. That means that, across the course of your career, you'll get to do maybe five long-term strategies, even if you stay a director for twenty-five years after a young start at 40.

Five.

They[4] reckon that it takes 10,000 hours of practice to master anything. So let's imagine that you put a hundred hours work into each strategy. That's quite a lot. That's pretty much three full weeks, working all day. Very few directors of any kind in any sizeable organisation get to dedicate so much time. But let's say a hundred. So, by the age of sixty-five, having started as a rising star at forty, you've now got five hundred hours strategy experience.

No wonder 90% of strategies fail. Actually, I feel that it's probably more like 99%.

This book proposes a different approach. Instead of waiting until you are invited up to the Board table, which may never happen anyway, why not set out to become a strategist now? How would you go about that?

My suggestion is that if you take a strategic approach to every problem you can find, you can clock up those hours rapidly, and you will do it much earlier in your career. Rather than waiting for the enormous problems to come along, I'm going to suggest that you can apply strategy to even ordinary problems throughout your working life.

---

4 Or, to be more exact, Malcolm Gladwell in Outliers, though he is so often cited that the figure is frequently taken to be a standard of some kind.

This doesn't mean you will be frantically going round with a clipboard 'strategising'. I'm going to offer you ten simple questions, which you can ask about anything. In most cases, merely asking those questions will give you insights you wouldn't otherwise have arrived at.

Strategy need not, and should not, be esoteric. Most strategy is obvious once you ask the right questions. The tragedy is that most organisational strategy proceeds not by asking any questions at all, but by bringing in some cumbersome and poorly understood strategic template, into which all of the real knowledge has to be shoehorned, destroying its usefulness in the process. In most cases, that template is the wrong one anyway. The result is what I'm going to call 'doomed strategy'.

If you can make five hours of the working day strategic (and, seriously, very few organisations will ask you to be 'less strategic' or to invest yourself in more unstrategic activities), then within ten years you will have clocked up 10,000 hours. Within six months you will have clocked up as many hours as most senior executives have by the time they retire. Six months.

Where are these strategy opportunities, then?

The day you start work in your first job, you should be able to take your job description and sketch out answers to the ten strategic questions. The first time you do it, you will be way off, but that's ok, because that creates an opportunity to redo the strategy when you learn a bit more, after you've watched how things play out. Start strategically, and your whole working experience will help you learn.

Every project you get handed, even if it's just planning the staff party, is an opportunity for strategy. Fairly soon, people will start to notice that you take a more complete approach to problems. You will start being asked into strategy meetings. While you're in a junior role, no one is going to welcome you turning up with an entirely different strategic plan, but you can ask one or more of the strategic questions. If the team has already got the answer, then you gain insight. If they haven't, your question could be saving your organisation a lot of problems. Don't expect to be rewarded straight away (you won't be) but these things get remembered. In time, you get a reputation as a 'lucky general'.

Ten minutes is, for most strategies, just the first sketch, but there will be occasions when you have to make a rapid series of decisions. Depending on what you do, these could be genuinely a matter of death or life. Practice makes perfect: find the opportunities to create, execute and evaluate strategy, even if (in fact, especially if) it all goes horribly wrong.

The ten strategic questions:

What is our situation?
What's the Big Idea?
Do we dare?
Who is with us?
What are we good at?
What are we doing that's different, and how will we take people with us?
What steps must we take, and in what order?
How do we get better as we go?
How are things arranged?
How will strategy change us?

What is strategy?

"Will somebody tell us what strategy actually is?" said Frank. Frank was aptly named, as he dared to say what everyone else was thinking. He had been co-opted onto a partnership board which actually had the word 'Strategic' in its title. I was the communications officer, and didn't have much of a say in things. The board had been talking around the question for several meetings, without ever offering an answer. Frank was a community leader, and so could play dumb if he wanted to.

What was astonishing (at the time—I would now almost expect it) is that no one around the table was actually able to give Frank an answer. The other members were, by and large, chief executives of extremely large organisations, there because they had proven themselves as they rose through the ranks. The average age was something like fifty-five, maybe sixty. Not only were they unable to give an answer, but they did not seem surprised that they couldn't. Strategy was one of those mysterious things, like jazz, that you could know when you heard it, but couldn't explain to anybody else.

Unfortunately, this is not unusual. The arcane and slightly mad way we go about recruiting for jobs in the Western world is largely to blame.

In your first job, unless you are a very high-flyer, or your uncle is the chair of the board, you start out doing mundane tasks which your degree in astrophysics or fractal mathematics has not really prepared you for. After a while, even if you are one of those rare people for whom pay is unimportant, you apply for a more senior job just to escape the monotony. If all goes well, you will carry on applying for more senior jobs for the rest of your working life. After a particular point, the job description will state that you are responsible for some kind of strategy. You will naturally include some mention of strategy in your résumé or CV. If you don't include some reference to it, you won't get an interview.

At the interview, you will be asked to give your thoughts on strategy. To do so, you will have quickly boned up, either by a cursory glance at a book ordered through Amazon Prime, or by speed-reading the Wikipedia page. You could actually spare yourself this step, because the person asking the question will have no more idea about strategy than you do. Too much reading may mark you as a geek.

Assuming you land the job, at some point you will be asked to present a strategy. This may scare you, until you realise that lurking in the paper files (if you still have them) or the file server, is the strategy that your predecessor devised, or, possibly, that a bunch of highly paid consultants wrote. You read that, adjust it a little, add in some things that are important to you and take out some things you don't like, and present it as a 'refresh' of the previously proven and effective strategy. All will be well, since no one on the Board will pay enough attention to criticise it, and your line manager will be happy that his or her own lack of strategic knowledge is not exposed.

At this point you might make a career-damaging error. You might actually go out and buy a book on strategy (or read the one you bought on Amazon a bit more carefully) and try to present an entirely new strategy based on your learning.

Unless that book was either this one, or Strategy Safari, then you are going to have a shock.

You walk into the Board meeting, and start to present your carefully crafted and lovingly made work of strategy, but after a couple of minutes, somebody snorts, stands up, and says 'that's not a strategy, because it doesn't contain a...'

What the 'a...' actually is depends on which book the complainant has read. It could be a Gantt chart, PERT diagram, budget, timeline, PESTLE, SWOT, or whatever it is that person thinks is the one true mark of strategy. They, like you, have read a book, and they may have built their entire corporate reputation on being 'the' strategist. But they only know about one kind of strategy, and if you didn't read the same book, then your strategy will be missing their magic ingredient.

However, in truth, there is no true magic ingredient.

So, what, then, is strategy?

Many strategy books begin (unhelpfully, in my opinion) by listing various things that are meant by the word, usually all beginning with 'P'.

Strategy is sometimes seen as a 'plan'. A plan is one kind of strategy, but it's not the only one, and it's not always appropriate.

Some see a strategy as a 'ploy'. Strategies can be built up around tactics, but they don't have to be.

Strategy is sometimes seen as a 'programme', which is especially unhelpful, because people also struggle to say exactly what a programme is.

Finally, strategy can also be seen as a 'pattern', an observed shape or behaviour in another organisation, which is quite possibly neither deliberate nor even self-understood.

Mintzberg, Ahlstrand and Lampel argue in Strategy Safari that there are actually ten entirely different schools of strategy, which is why we are talking, frequently, about ten totally different things. Most of this book will be about exploring those ten schools, but we will start with a working definition which we can explain to someone else without having to go through all ten.

Strategy, in its simplest form, is a better way to get from A to B. To do strategy means to consider at least one alternative to the 'obvious' or 'bulldozer' approach, and to the 'residual' approach, which is to say, doing what the organisation always does.

Strategy: finding a better way to get from A to B.

In The Horse and His Boy, by C.S. Lewis, adventurers Aravis, Shasta and their (talking) horses Bree and Hwin decide to take a different route across the desert. Instead of going via the Oasis, they head for a narrow gorge in which they will be able to find water.

When they arrive at the gorge, they want to take it easy, at first believing that they have found a faster way than their enemies. But, as they discover, the route was not faster, but (for other reasons) better. Read the book for yourself, if you haven't already: it is a masterwork of strategy.

'Better' can cover a lot of things. Better could be safer, it could be cheaper, it could be the optimal combination of cost and performance, it could result in additional goals being reached, or hard-to-obtain resources being conserved for future projects. The point is that it requires consideration of an alternative. It could be that this consideration leads you back to the obvious or the residual approach, which is 'doing what we always do'. There is no benefit in doing something clever for its own sake. Nonetheless, in the words of an ancient proverb: 'It is the wisdom of the wise to give thought to their ways', or, to paraphrase Socrates, 'the unexamined path is not worth pursuing'.

Let's therefore consider the three irremovable aspects of strategy: 'A', 'B', and 'to'.

A is where you are starting from. You have to know where you are now. This does not need to be exhaustive, but it does need to involve knowledge of the key details. Is money going to be an issue? Then you need to know the budget, and any strictures on spending it. Are you facing resentment from certain quarters? That's part of A. Is there some danger heading down the tracks? That's also part of A.

B is where you are going. Has this been agreed? In my analysis of failed strategy, failure to agree what the ultimate intention is, is one of the crucial factors. You do not need to pin this down completely, as we will see later, but you need to have some sense of 'how will we know when it's done'. As well as setting the direction, this gives an idea of value. When involved in a war of national survival, 'not losing' is so important that all of the resources of the nation can be directed to it. On the other hand, if the goal is to attend a birthday party, there comes a point at which you have to say 'it isn't worth it'.

'To' is the route you take. Even if you are considering a physical journey, this route is still partly a metaphorical one. It can mean a series of steps, but it could also mean a set of practised responses to situations. It can include deciding how you pick the music in the car, or how you will choose what to do when you encounter an unplanned diversion.

What causes strategy?

Some people will ask: why have a strategy at all? When do you need strategy, as opposed to merely carrying on with what you always do.

Strategy is generally caused by situation, or ambition.

Most people and most organisations happily keep doing what they're doing without considering strategy, until one of two things happen. Either the situation changes in such a way that what they're doing no longer works, or they develop new ambitions.

Ambition-based strategy can be dangerous, because it may put the organisation at risk when there was no need for it, but organisations without ambition are in danger of becoming increasingly irrelevant in a changing environment.

Strategy is not the inevitable result of either of these things. A changing situation often leads to organisational stubbornness. Ambition can lead to a rise in wishful thinking, with wild forays into the unknown. Strategy can be dangerous, but in the face of a changing situation or ambitious leadership, not having a strategy is far more dangerous.

Ensuring that your strategy is one of the successful ones is the subject of the next chapter.

Why strategies fail

I said earlier that one, possibly tendentious, estimate is that 90% of strategies fail. But why do they fail?

First, strategies fail because they are not implemented.

Second, strategies fail because they are doomed by their own logical flaws.

Third, strategies fail because they succumb to internal resistance.

Fourth, strategies fail because they are overwhelmed by external circumstances.

We'll take these in order.

Failure to implement

If you reach a fork in the road, and you can't remember whether your strategy says go left or go right, then you don't have a strategy. Organisational strategies are usually ridiculously complex. This makes them cumbersome, which is a problem in itself, and it can also make it hard to identify logical flaws, but the biggest problem of complexity is simply that the people tasked with implementing them can't remember what they are supposed to do.

When people can't remember what to do, they do one of four things.

By far the most common is that they return to residual strategy, the default behaviour of the organisation. It is expressed often in mantras such as 'the customer is king' or 'it's a jungle out there'. When the default strategy is war, peace will be hard to obtain. When the default strategy is cost-cutting, money to invest will be hard to find.

The second is that they take the bulldozer approach, the 'obvious'. What is obvious varies from person to person. To some people, it is obvious that you should treat the customer like royalty. To others, it is obvious that giving the customer too much help creates expectations which can't be fulfilled.

The third is that they act based on misunderstanding or mis-remembering. This can be comic, but it has long-term consequences, embedding a caricature into organisational culture.

The fourth is that they act counter-rationally. Their memory of the strategy is only that it appears to go against common sense. Therefore, in trying to obey the strategy, they do that which goes against common sense.

To avoid this, all that is necessary is to have strategies which are simple enough to explain, and to ensure that you do explain them simply.

Doomed

Some strategies are doomed from the beginning because of their internal weaknesses. A strategy which has been hammered out as a compromise between two powerful interests may be meant as a best-of-both-worlds solution, but, as often as not, it simply glosses over fundamental flaws. These issues are not hard to spot for those who look carefully, but often the corporate pressure is in the direction of not looking.

Tell-tales signs of this are when words are used in different ways throughout a strategy document, when sections appear as if randomly placed, when goals are articulated in quite different ways, and when there appears to be a too strict demarcation between different functions within the organisation. If strategy is a better way to get from A to B, then 'strategic' refers to the whole of the organisation's resources being directed to achieve all of the organisation's goals.

True logical errors require more work to identify. You have to follow through the necessary consequences of the elements of the strategy. In a certain sense, any strategy which is actually implemented and is not interrupted by externals will 'succeed', which is to say it will cause the logical consequences of the combination of actions taken, but those consequences may be far from the intentions of the planners. Obvious logical errors include finances not adding up, resources assigned to be in two places at once, and events planned to take place before the steps which cause them. More subtle issues include such things as perverse incentives, when the declared strategy of the organisation is one thing, but the incentives given to staff are the opposite, and undeclared premises, where implicit but undeclared assumptions run counter to each other.

At the root of many doomed strategies is the wrong strategic template. A planning strategy is excellent if you want to build a house, but almost certain to fail if you are fighting a war. A political strategy could be excellent to gain backing for your fundraising campaign, but, stuck up a mountain with two candles and no tent, it is not going to help.

Resisted

Strategies often fail because of a lack of engagement by those meant to implement them.

Blunt **defiance** is uncommon, though it gets a lot of publicity, perhaps as a conflict between shareholders and the board, or between unions and management, or between supplier and customer.

Wait and See is a natural tendency: we like to hedge our bets. A certain amount of Wait and See is inevitable, but if people are still waiting when their engagement is needed, the project will fail.

Pseudo-adoption is when people appear to be following the strategy, but are in fact only following it in as much as it satisfies their other agendas.

Labelling is when, by malice or mistake, a group simply labels what it currently does with the words from the new strategy. In my experience, labelling is by far the most pervasive.

Defiance: Explicit Opposition	**Wait and See:** Delay until satisfied
Pseudo-Adoption: Going along with parts of the strategy for own purposes	**Labelling:** Redescribing current activity with the new words, so nothing changes

Apart from explicit defiance, all of these can appear to be simple misunderstandings or the result of pressure of work. We should, of course, always try to use 'best case analysis', where we attribute the most noble motivations to the actions of others. However, in the words of a famous teacher, we need to be 'as wise as snakes, while being as innocent as doves'. Most organisations have staff or volunteers who have become skillful in creating an impression of complying while secretly opposing. Often they believe they are doing so with the best of motives— to protect the organisation from risk, to stop too much power going to unproven leaders, to press on with what they believe to be the real purpose of the organisation, and so on.

Leaving those aside, why do people resist strategy? Fundamentally, strategy causes change. If people are comfortable with what they are currently doing, they will generally be reluctant to change it. If people are already afraid in their current situation, they are likely to be afraid of change—even if that change would benefit them. People with a vested interest in the current system may oppose change, even if that change would produce direct advantages for them. An example of this is when everyone is offered a pay upgrade to the same level. It is to everyone's advantage to take the pay increase, but the staff who were previously on a higher rate than other staff will often oppose it, because they have a vested interest in the pay differential.

People also resist strategy because of issues of territory. A strategy which will improve logistics may be heavily resisted if it comes from the branding team. Even if the proposal would help them, the 'not invented here' tendency can mean they will resist it.

Scarcity mentality is another reason for resisting strategy. While others may agree in principle with the reason for the strategy, and they may even agree with the methods, they see it as taking away resources—people, money, equipment, buildings, even something as intangible as organisational attention—from the programme they want to run.

Overwhelmed

Except in Chess, Draughts and Connect Four, strategy is always subject to unexpected external influences. Even in games such as chess, which have no chance element, strategists have to work in the knowledge that there is an opposing strategist intent on neutralising their strategy.

Time	Resources	Regulation	Requirement	Reputation

Five elements that can overwhelm.

What kinds of external circumstances are we talking about?

The most important is simply the passage of time. Almost everything in the world around us alters. There are long term trends which will eventually invalidate most of the assumptions strategists make. This is one reason why simply refreshing an old strategy could be inviting disaster. There are also short term fluctuations. If you're running an ice-cream business, a cold summer could see it collapse.

Then there are changes in the availability of resources. The advent of the Lottery in the UK during the 1990s saw millions of pounds poured into the construction industry for major capital projects in the arts, sport and heritage. One unexpected and unintended result of this was that the availability of plasterers and bricklayers dropped. This pushed up the price of all the projects.

Changes in regulation can also cause problems. If you rely on volunteers from abroad, a change in visa processes can capsize what you are doing. A minor revision to labelling regulations could make your entire line of goods unsaleable.

A change in the requirements of your customers can invalidate your strategy. This is not just about commercial customers. If you are a regiment fighting in a major war, then a peace agreement will certainly mean an end to your current programme. If the peace is long-lasting and stable, it may mean an end to your regiment.

Finally, something as intangible as reputation can break your strategy. Failing to manage what people are saying about you—even if there is no truth in it—can mean that your suppliers stop supplying you, your donors stop giving, your customers stop buying, and the government steps in to stop you operating.

There is hope

If strategies are so apt to fail, should we embark on them at all? Even the very best strategy can be scuppered by one or more of these things, but, by and large, good strategists build these risks into strategy. This is another reason why it's worth getting all the strategic practice you possibly can: after a while, likely problems become obvious to you. What's more, when the worst comes to the worst, you can be finalising an entirely new strategy while others are still wringing their hands about the old one.

Strategy Safari name	10 Minute STRATEGIST name	Strategic Question
Environmental	Situation	What is our situation?
Cognitive	Thinking	What's the Big Idea?
Entrepreneurial	Resolve	Do we dare?
Political	Allies	Who is with us?
Positioning	Tactics	What are we good at?
Cultural	Embedding	What are we doing that's different, and how will we take people with us?
Planning	Gameplan	What steps must we take, and in what order?
Learning	Improvements	How do we get better as we go?
Design	Systems	How are things arranged?
Transformational	Transformation	How will strategy change us?

If you are reading both books, this table shows how our terminology links with Strategy Safari's. If you aren't, you can safely ignore it.

1 Situation

We are now going to get into the meat of the 10 Minute Strategist. We have ten areas to look at, which, helpfully, form the acronym 'STRATEGIST'. These correspond to the ten strategic schools which we referred to on page 7. We've structured them in this order because this (we believe) is a good order for asking the questions. It also makes a logical order for presenting a strategy, though, watch out—in most cases you just need to give the 'big idea', and you may lose people's interest if you try to explain in too much depth how you got there.

The ten points are iterative, which is to say that once you've gone all the way through, you will probably change what you put down at the start.

For a ten minute strategy, expect to spend about a minute on each one. If you're doing a two day strategy workshop, you'll want to go into more depth. If spending three months for a five year plan, there's yet more to do. We'll break it down into those three chunks as we go.

Strategic question 1: What is our situation?

Whether you're doing the ten minute, two day or three month version, begin with this simple question: "What is our situation?" You can also say "Where are we now?" or "What's it like?" or even "Why are we having this conversation?"

If you're going to follow this in Strategy Safari, the Situation question goes with the Environmental school of strategy, though we're not going to adopt that fully. Essentially, the Environmental school says that strategy is the result of environment, and that organisations are forced to evolve in particular ways by that environment. People in this school tend to be academics observing strategy, rather than practitioners doing deliberate strategy. Even so it's the right place to start: you cannot possibly come up with an effective strategy unless you know where you are beginning. This is the 'A' of 'A to B'.

10 minute version

In the ten minute version, we are asking and answering based on what we already know. So, if you are going to spend one minute on understanding the situation, get a pen and paper, and sketch out your best approximation. Don't try to be exhaustive—look just for the 'salient' points. Salient, in this context, means things which are part of the reason you are doing a strategy at all.

Let's take a real life example.[5]

---

5 All the examples in this book actually happened, but we've simplified them for the book. They are not 'proofs' that it works, but illustrations of how to do it. For this reason, we've left out all the names and any other ways the stories could be identified. If you know the stories, or think you do, feel free to chuckle knowingly, but please treat them as fictional examples.

You have just taken over as the national director of a voluntary organisation at your annual team retreat in Luxembourg. After an enjoyable day of walking in the great outdoors, one of the team comes to you and says that her son is missing, and so is the son of another team member. Where you are is Luxembourg's 'Little Switzerland': beautiful landscape, but full of caves, cliffs, steep slopes and covered in forest. You might be tempted to hand back control to your predecessor, but it is in fact your predecessor's son who is the other child missing.

So, what are the salient facts of your situation? You ask a couple of questions, and discover the following:

- Contrary to instructions, neither of the missing boys has their phone, and they apparently won't know the name, address or number of the place you are staying
- The area where they went missing is in the same woodland where your camp is, surrounded by road on all sides
- Two of your team members are experienced in outdoor search and rescue
- If you call the police, they will ask you to wait twenty-four hours before they take action
- The parents are too emotionally involved to take part in anything constructive
- You have a number of vehicles and drivers
- You have a total of thirty team members. None of them speak Luxemburgish.
- You have several mobile phones, and the signal appears generally good
- You have maps.

All this you can scribble down in a minute, at least in note form. This is your situation. There is no time to conduct exhaustive analysis of the political, economic, social and legal environments, and it's unlikely that it would help anyway.

At this point, you don't need to draw any conclusions, though some conclusions will probably have presented themselves. Just get the salient facts. Jot them down: the clock is ticking.

Two day version

In the two day version, you will have time to spend an entire hour on situation, so you will expect to go deeper. Clearly, you could not possibly take two days on the missing children problem we just discussed. A two day workshop is suited to 20 to 40 days of strategy execution. In most organisations, 20 to 40 days of direct execution could take you a whole year.

Nonetheless, an hour is not an enormous amount of time, so you will need to move briskly.

There are several situation tools out there. The most popular and famous of them is the SWOT analysis, which stands for 'Strengths, Weaknesses, Opportunities, Threats'. SWOT was enormously popular in the 1980s and 1990s, though its inherent weaknesses are now more apparent. SWOT properly belongs to the Design school of strategy, which comes under our 'Systems' heading, so leave the SWOT analysis for now.

A more helpful tool is the PESTLES analysis. This just gives a series of headings which help to organise your thoughts.

Practically speaking, get together a group of about six people with insights into what you need to do and why you need to do it.

The temptation is to collect the six most senior people in your team or organisation, but you really want to do everything you can to have 'thought diversity'. Thought diversity is not the same as race, gender and religion representation. It's possible to have a group who come from different ethnic backgrounds, are mixed gender and have entirely different religious or philosophical backgrounds, and yet who all think identically as regards your strategy because they've been through the same company training programme.

If you have six people, try to include someone who is new to the organisation, try to include someone who is a front-line worker (whatever the front line is in your business), and try to include someone who has been with the organisation a long time, even if in a relatively junior position. If you have a mix of senior people and junior people, which is best, you need to make it clear before you begin that everyone is being asked to contribute equally to the discussion, that no ideas are stupid ideas, and that no one's career or annual assessment depends on what happens in the room. You are going to play by 'Chatham House' rules, which means that you can take away anything that anyone said in the meeting, but you can't attribute it to them.

Get a whiteboard or flip chart, and put down the following headings:

> Political
> Economic
> Social
> Technological
> Legal
> Ecological
> Spiritual

For each one of them, spend about five minutes asking people to call out aspects of your current situation which they think are relevant to 'strategy'. If they ask you to define the goals first, tell them that you want to leave things open for now—you will come to it in the next section: if you define them now, you will skew the conversation.

Political includes the politics of the country or countries you are in, local politics, and even internal company politics. It's fine for people to laugh a little bit, but you need to prevent it from becoming an opportunity for political humour. When discussing internal politics, ask people to avoid naming specific persons if they can. It's not that this isn't important, it's just that you are liable to end up in a fight if rival factions are present in the meeting.

Economic includes the macro-economic situation of the nation, but also the micro-economic situation of your industry, your company, even your business unit. If you're a charity, NGO or other not-for-profit, you might talk about the fund-raising environment.

Social is about the intangible aspects of society. You might talk about language issues, class issues, social trends, attitudes and values. As before, this includes national, local, and internal.

Technological is usually about new technological developments. These currently move very fast. You want to avoid getting into a technological debate. If two people disagree, write down both points of view.

Legal is about law, and especially about changes in the law which may be on their way. This section can tend to degenerate into a conversation about 'what the law ought to be'. You may need to remind people that you are only concerned with what is, and what is on its way, not what ought.

Ecological was added to the PESTLE structure relatively recently. What about climate change? What about changes in environmental regulation, such as congestion charging or low-emissions zones in cities?

Finally, I have added '**Spiritual**' to cover a range of issues which modern people rarely discuss. This includes aspirations, hopes, fears and the bigger existential questions, as well as matters of mental health, romance and the arts. Without the spiritual, we have only a bleak and monochrome picture of the world we are in.

This should have taken thirty-five minutes. Take five minutes to summarise by underlining the issues that the group agrees (or you think) are most significant. For significance, read 'either part of the problem, or possibly part of the solution'. Mere information about what's out there on its own does not generate strategy, though it may be that something that was logged in passing becomes significant later on.

Forty minutes of your hour have now passed. Move on to Brand Analysis. A brand is a promise of an experience, and every organisation, programme,product and individual has one, even if it doesn't know or care. Your brand is made up of three things which you control, and one thing which you don't.

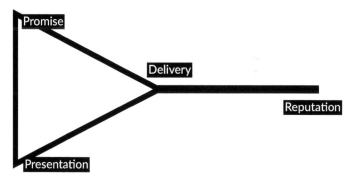

Brand analysis
How people perceive your brand is shaped by your Promise and Presentation, but it is determined by your record of Delivery. Over-presenting and over-promising will not compensate for inconsistent delivery.

In terms of control, brand is what you **promise**, what you **deliver**, and how you **present** this promise. Mostly, when people talk about brand, they are talking about presentation, and they think about logos, colours, typefaces and websites. In fact, none of that is worth anything unless you actually promise something which people are interested in, which generally means that you are promising to solve a problem which they recognise they have. That promise is only as good as your delivery. Consistently

31

fulfil your promise, and your brand is valuable. Fail to deliver, even if only occasionally, and your brand dies.

What you don't control is what people say about your brand. This is your **reputation**. You can do some things, through Public Relations and social media, to help manage your reputation, but, ultimately, the best reputation you can possibly have is the one that aligns exactly with what you really are. If you engage in lots of marketing activity to get yourself a better reputation than you deserve, you will end up disappointing a lot of people and the result ultimately will be a worse reputation than you started with.

This brand analysis can take fifteen minutes. You just want to get the key points down, so urge people not to talk about what the brand ought to be, just about what it actually is. If you're not a commercial organisation, you may think you don't have a brand, or the brand you have is unimportant to your strategy. Rather than labour the point, get people to focus on reputation.

You have five minutes left. You could do you yet another summary, but you're in danger of 'death by feedback'. So just lay the flip chart sheets on the floor, or get people to look at the whiteboard or whatever else you're using, and ask two questions. First, is there anything really important and obvious which is missing? Second, ask them to summarise in just one sentence (they can each write their own sentence down and then read it out) what your overall situation is. Job done. Have a coffee break.

Three month version

If you are putting together a five year plan for an organisation, then you will probably want to spend a couple of weeks gathering information from across the organisation. This will include desk research, such as reading annual reports, interviews with specialists, and at least two or three meetings like the one outlined above. However, you should beware the tendency to merely catalogue and categorise what is already there. At the end of the process, you should be in a position to succinctly describe the various activities and organisational units, in such a way that the people involved with them recognise themselves. But you should also seek to understand the information in new ways. This is often a question of combining different kinds of information, for example:

Maps

You can now produce maps of geographical data quite easily using freely available online mapping tools, or GIS software. If you are in a large organisation, there is probably someone already equipped with this and trained in it: it will take much less time to ask them to help you out. Mapping information which has previously only been shown in tables can give you new insights.

Graphs

Most organisations produce graphs of their performance, and for larger organisations this is often keyed as a part of a database. Is it possible to produce graphs of something other than mere financial returns? You need to be careful with this kind of thing, and you should get help from a statistician if you have not been trained in managing statistics, but one effective graph may be enough to transform your whole approach.

Opinion surveys

You can conduct an internal opinion survey using Survey-Monkey or other online and offline tools, many of which (such as LimeSurvey) are available for free. Ideally your opinion survey should grow out of questions that came up as a result of the information you've been gathering. Resist the temptation to start the survey until you know what you're asking.

Focus groups

A focus group is a facilitated group of people brought together for their insights on a particular set of questions. Running one or more focus groups can generate a great deal of creative input. To make the most out of focus groups, have them led by someone who is not affected by what the group says. Otherwise there will inevitably be a degree of social pressure in one direction or the other. The point of a focus group is to focus further research: everything you get from them is opinion, not fact. They can be highly useful for generating ideas, but don't base your strategy on the information they provide.

Public information

Vast amounts of information are now available for free online. They are typically in formats such as .SHP shapefiles or .KML files which can easily be imported into mapping software, or else as keyed .CSV files. Many organisations do not make use of this data.

With all of the information inputs you have, the biggest task is selection and organisation. What are the salient facts? Rather than obsessing over what to include and what to leave out, go on to the rest of the strategy and come back to the Situation when you have finished. Doing the rest of the work may throw up additional questions you need answered.

For now, after you've gathered the initial situation information, write down an answer to the following two questions:

"What will happen if we don't change what we do?" and

"What could happen if we did?"

From there, proceed to the next section: Thinking.

2 Thinking

Thinking reflects the Cognitive school of strategy. In some ways, this is almost the opposite of the Environmental school we looked at under Situation. The Environmentalists say 'what does our situation push us into?' The Cognitivists say 'let us dream of what could be'.

Essentially, for this section, we want to think differently and creatively about what we are trying to achieve, and how we might achieve it. This section is as much about deciding which goals to pursue as about finding a clever way of reaching them.

The key is creativity. If we stick with the old thought patterns, we will produce something very similar to the old answers.

How do these thought patterns work? Often they are expressed in little phrases, such as 'it's a jungle out there', or they are inherent in organisational structures or the agendas of meetings.

In one organisation I worked for, 'Communications', which was my area, was ninth on every committee agenda, ostensibly to ensure that Communications was always discussed. The actual result was that Communications was never discussed, because the other agenda points overran, and Communications was given two minutes before 'Date and Time of Next Meeting'. After reviewing our departmental strategy, we informed everyone that we would no longer be attending committee meetings unless specifically required there for a main agenda item, and committees should send someone to see us when they wanted our help. We found that, in a team of five, we saved more than fifteen hours a week. Productivity went up, boredom went down.

Existing thought patterns are sometimes expressed in mission statements, vision statements, lists of corporate values, and in the stories told about how the organisation came to be and what it is for.

Strategic question 2: What's the Big Idea?

The underlying question in Thinking is 'What's the Big Idea?' Sometimes simply defining the situation puts the big idea into your head. If not, one good way to approach it is to say 'what if?'

In the film 'The Seven Samurai'[6], villagers notice that bandits have come to spy out their territory, but the bandits do not attack. The villagers report this to the elders, and the elders note that the bandits will not attack until the crops are gathered. Then they will take everything and kill the villagers, unless they flee. This is inevitable, given the power of the bandits versus the power of the villagers. This is an excellent example of 'old' thought patterns.

The villagers then go to the oldest man in the village, and ask for his advice. He tells them that when he was a small child,

6 Akira Kurosawa, 1954. Remade in English as the The Magnificent Seven, 1960, and numerous other imitations.

fleeing after just such a raid, he saw another village where people did not flee. That village had hired Samurai to defend them.

From there, the villagers decide to pursue the same strategy. We shall come back to this at the end of the book.

In their case, the what-if question is "what if this was not inevitable?" in other words, what if we don't flee? What would have to happen for us not to flee?

It's interesting to note that they go to a much older person to get a new idea. New ideas are not necessarily the province of the young. It's also worth noting that the old man expressed his thoughts in the idea of a narrative. This can be very helpful: tell the story of how things are going to work. This story is, in essence, your strategy.

10 minute version

In a single minute, what new thought can you bring to a problem? A single minute is plenty, if you think intentionally.

Use these three questions:

First, is there something which is 'above challenge' that you can challenge? What if you changed the goals? What if you ignored one of the key parameters? What if you took a barrier and turned it into a bridge?

Second, is there something which jumps out at you from the Situation as an opportunity? Is there some overlooked piece of information which came to light? As you practice strategy, you will get used to spotting those nuggets of insight which hide in a mass of data.

Third, is there a way you can re-narrate, as the villagers do in The Seven Samurai? One of the biggest problems for creativity in strategy is the notion that the situation you are in has only an inevitable outcome. What would Batman do in this situation, or Buffy, or the Pope, or Lizzy Bennett from Pride and Prejudice? Consider the most sensible option, and reverse it.

All of these are ways of doing 'what if?', and you will develop your own as you practise strategy.

To go back to our example of the boys lost in the Luxembourg woods, consider this insight: why did the boys get lost? You could say they were young boys, and that's what young boys do, but there is a 'why?' behind everything. They surely got lost because they carried on walking and missed the way. What are they likely to do? The answer: continue walking. The inevitable consequence of keeping walking is that you run out of woodland. Although large, the area was constrained by road, and the boys would, unless incapacitated, eventually come out at the road. Of course, they could encounter other adventures along the way, but the most likely outcome is that they will hit the road. This gives us the germ of a strategic idea, and we will look at that in the next section.

Two day version

In your two day workshop, you've had coffee after the Situation session. People are buoyed up by the fact that they actually had fun in the first session, and that it finished on time. You now bring them back for the 'creative bit'.

The problem with asking groups for creative ideas is that they immediately begin to lock themselves down into uncreative ones. Someone suggests that you have to have SMART goals (more on that later). Somebody else suggests that you need to build measurement and evaluation in from the start. Someone suggests that, no matter how good the ideas are, the organisation will smother them, as it did in... (cue a long story about something that happened several years before).

Begin, therefore, by telling people that the session they are entering will be unlike any session they have previously taken part in. You are not going to use SMART goals, you are going to explore CLEVER goals. We'll explain them in just a moment. Tell them you are looking for the radically creative, the madcap, the barely plausible.[7]

This will take five minutes. You can profitable use the next ten minutes by reviewing what was discussed in the Situation session, and asking if anything stands out. What stands out could be an opportunity, an insight, or something that doesn't fit. Don't press the point. If nothing jumps out, let the thoughts ferment while you go on to the next idea.

You've now used fifteen minutes. If by this time you've got a radical new idea which seems like it could be your strategy, the temptation is to jump to the end and start to evaluate it. Don't do this. Hold your nerve.

For the next fifteen minutes, play 'what if'. What if you were to remove one of the key parameters identified in situation? What if you were to double one (whatever that means in your context)? Again, if you come up with a plausible answer, or if you come up with no answer, keep going.

Half your session has now gone. That's great.

Now outline the 'obvious', 'default' or 'bulldozer' approach. What's the obvious answer which everybody already thought of, or is what your organisation always does, or is the one that could be achieved if only you threw enough resources at it? Often you will know what this is before you began, but it might help if you ask one of the group to describe it. Allow them a maximum of five minutes, otherwise the explanation is too long. Record it in some form on the whiteboard or flipchart.

---

7 Sometimes for these kind of sessions someone suggests 'think the unthinkable'. This is unhelpful for two reasons. First, it is literally impossible, and, second, people often take it to mean 'allow yourself to propose things otherwise morally reprehensible'. We are looking for creative ideas, not nasty ideas.

For the next ten minutes, lead the group through 'what if we did the opposite?' for each stage of the obvious solution. Of course, in most cases, there will not be a realistic single opposite, but that doesn't matter, as long as the people in the group are willing to propose opposites. The opposite game is just a method of freeing up creative capacity.

You now have fifteen minutes left. Take five of them to explain what CLEVER goals are.

SMART goals, as almost everyone knows, are Specific, Measurable, Agreed (or, according to some, Achievable), Realistic and Timed[8]. They're great when it comes to a project plan, but useless when it comes to creative strategy. So, instead, use CLEVER.

CLEVER goals are:

Creative—you are looking for alternatives to the obvious goals.

Loose ended—at this stage, you do not need to wrap up exactly what they mean. You will have to revise them later anyway as you continue the strategy process, so tidying them now is just wasting time.

Emergent—they grow as you go. Although we are putting a solid hour of creative thinking in right now, we will continue to let the goals grow and mature, and maybe change, as we work through the rest of the process.

Valuable—the funny thing about SMART goals is that they contain no suggestion that the goals should actually be important. This is because SMART is a method for formatting goals, not for generating them. CLEVER goals are goals which do something you really want.

---

8 SMART was first proposed by George T. Doran in There's a S.M.A.R.T. way to write management's goals and objectives, The Management Review, November 1981, There are several versions in current use.

Easy—goals need to be easy. They either need to be easy for you, or you need to find the person or organisation for whom they are easy, or you have to break them down into easy chunks. When it comes to making a plan, you will proceed through a series of goals until you finally reach the desired result. If any of those goals are too hard, then you either run the risk of missing them and thus failing the entire programme, or else you will over-invest, and possibly fail at some other, easier goal.

Repeatable—working out how to do something the first time is tricky. If you can figure a way to do it repeatably, then you can turn it into a Tactic, which we will look at later. If one of your intermediate goals is 'get a plumber', then including repeatability in the goal means that if, later, you need to add another plumber, or your original plumber quits or goes off sick, you now already have a method of doing it.

With your final ten minutes, ask them to identify what might be some CLEVER goals that will be stepping stones to achieving your final result.

So, an hour has gone by. But you haven't evaluated what you've come up with. Don't worry, that is coming in the next section.

Three month version

For a three month strategy formation process, draw a picture. This picture is your 'strategic model' (at least, it is when you tell people about it—to begin with, it's just a picture). This is a picture of what you think the problem, and the situation, and the end goal is like. You'll want to have several goes at it on your own, perhaps aided by a session like the one we just looked at. Do not use Microsoft Word Art. In fact, to begin with, don't use any software at all. It's just you, and a pad of paper, and some coloured pens. You may have seen strategic models before which look like temples or houses. If you've seen these, make a point to draw nothing like a temple or a house. How is the problem like a dragon? How is the situation like a waterfall? How is it like a box of chocolates? How is it like someone's video collection? Keep coming up with random ideas until you find a picture which actually seems to make some sense.

The next thing to do is to tour the picture. Make appointments with as many people as possible. Draw the picture out for them (don't take a previously printed copy with you). Get them to add things, delete things, change things. If they come up with a better picture, start to use that one as well, or instead.

As you tour your picture, you will find yourself having to narrate it. People want a story which runs on the lines of 'this happens, and because of it, that happens, and because of that… ' Telling the story will impact the picture, and changing the picture will impact the story. Try to talk with twenty people at different levels in your organisation. If your organisation is smaller than that, then try talking to well-wishers, supporters or customers. If you don't have enough of those to make up the twenty, try stopping random people in the park, or making an appointment with a local politician.

It doesn't actually matter if the people you share it with improve it. Every time you tell it and show it to someone else, you are improving it. At a particular point, creative insight will take over (it always does), and you will make some kind of radical tweak.

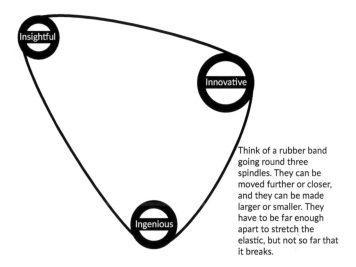

Think of a rubber band going round three spindles. They can be moved further or closer, and they can be made larger or smaller. They have to be far enough apart to stretch the elastic, but not so far that it breaks.

How do you know when to stop?

When I'm asked to evaluate strategies, I always look for what I call 'the clever bit'. I want to see the part that is innovative, insightful and ingenious.

Innovative—it's not just a repeat of what's been done before.

Insightful—the idea helps me understand the problem better.

Ingenious—there is some genuine 'going round the back' thinking involved.

Use this 'three Ins' test to determine if you should keep thinking, or move on to the next section. Remember, though, that even if you fully pass the test, your idea is only a provisional one until you've completed the full STRATEGIST list. Always be ready to come back to any part and change everything if you have to.

3 Resolve

The Entrepreneurial school of strategy focusses on the role of the leader as strategist. It is about the big boss with the big idea, the Napoleon, Alexander or Caesar. Developing the leadership qualities of the leader is a strategy in itself. Stephen Covey's 7 Habits of Highly Effective People[9] is a seminal example of trying to build strategy into the character of the leader.

To some extent, we would concur. Indeed, this entire book is about getting you to practise being a strategist.

One of the reasons for the popularity of this school is that individual leaders are often seen to be more effective than committees, boards and organisational hierarchies. They are decisive, show resolve, and, by force of personality, carry off strategies which might not otherwise work.

The problem for most would-be strategists is that there are very few situations where you are allowed to behave in this way.

9 The 7 Habits of Highly Effective People. Restoring the Character Ethic, Covey, Stephen R., The Business Library, 1996.

Political parties, publicly traded companies, sports clubs, arts societies, church denominations and government bodies are all organised to prevent a single powerful, albeit visionary, leader from taking control and potentially wrecking everything.

How, then, do we apply the entrepreneurial character to a board or executive committee which has been designed to thwart it?

Strategic question 3: Do we dare?

What are we going to do, what's it going to cost, and what are we going to get out of it? These are, of course, the questions that Bilbo Baggins wants answers to at the start of The Hobbit. Resolve is all about being ready to do it, whatever it is. Courage is needed, but not blind courage. We look before we leap.

You can keep the question in your own mind, but don't put it like that out loud, else you'll scare off the people you're trying to persuade. To help your non-Napoleons take on a little bit of the mantle of the old emperor, you will need to break it down into five areas.

- Results
- Resources
- Risks
- Resistance
- Rewards

Your intention is to bring a committee, or perhaps just a dithering boss, to the point of making a decision like they were Napoleon.

The first thing you need to be able to explain is exactly what results you are seeking to achieve. This is the point at which you SMARTen up your CLEVER.

Think of it this way: the CLEVER part of your strategy is a rather ambling, scattily dressed creative genius who has come up with a superb way to get to what everybody wants. The problem is, if he walks into your Board meeting, half the members will try to give him some money to buy a cup of tea, and the other half will call security. You need to put him in a suit, shirt and tie, and make sure that all the shirt buttons are done up properly and that his shoes are polished.

So, you take your Creative, Loose-ended, Emergent, Valuable, Easy and Repeatable set of goals, and you format them as Specific, Measurable, Achievable, Realistic and Timed. Don't worry that you may need to change them later. Your Board, committee or dithering boss will almost certainly insist that you review them anyway.

You are effectively going to these people and saying what is for them the most comforting thing: "Judge me by my results". There is nothing quite like that for these groups, which are used to presentations by people who are already digging an escape tunnel before the project even starts. Vanishingly few project proposals talk about results. The better ones focus on the problem and the steps they want to take, the 'A' and 'to', but rarely are there people confident enough to actually declare their intended results up front.

You then need to talk about Resources. What is it going to cost to get these results? The Board, committee or boss wants to decide for themselves if it's actually worth it. Resources, in these terms, include money, people, equipment, premises, and intangibles such as 'opportunity cost', which is the opportunities you lose by pursuing this strategy as opposed to another one, or just hanging around hoping something will happen.

You'll have most Boards in your hand after you've given these two, but you need to go on to the rest if you want them to truly act with the Resolve that you need.

Risks come in three kinds: the **risks that come with doing nothing,** the **risks to the strategy while it's executing,** and the **risks which success itself generates.** You are not trying to scare the Board (etc) here, but you need to be clear about what can go wrong.

There are elaborate systems for rating risks based on likelihood and impact[10], and if your audience is used to these then you should use them, but don't try to introduce them if they aren't already understood.

Let's unpick them for a moment:

Risk of doing nothing, which is the same as the risk of pursuing the obvious or default strategy: it is what will happen if you don't take the strategic route you are proposing, or another similarly innovative, insightful and ingenious approach. Do not try to go too far with these. They should be 'obviously true'. Quite possibly the reason you are being allowed to propose a strategy is because the decision-makers are already aware of them. Keep it factual, and dry.

Risks to the strategy are the externals that you can't control. If you want your strategy to be accepted, you need to show that

---

10 See page 55, Risk Matrix.

you have thought about them, and have a way of minimising their likelihood, or their impact, or both. If questioned, don't be afraid to say 'at that point, the strategy would fail' if they begin to propose highly unlikely situations. Most decision-makers want to know that you are capable of countenancing failure. "Nothing can go wrong" is not a phrase that inspires confidence in the kinds of people who get onto committees.

Risks of success are what can happen if the project is too successful. I was once called in to run an advertising campaign for a food co-operative that wished to expand its operations. The way advertising campaigns work is that you can't stop them once they've started. It can be like triggering an avalanche. So I asked the co-operative leaders to explain how they would handle things if sales doubled, if they quadrupled, if they increased ten-fold, and so on. They assured me that they had processes in place for all these eventualities.

We ran the campaign, and sales doubled within a week. In the second week, the paid employee who ran the co-operative went off sick with stress, and everything ground to a halt: she had not understood the risks of success.

Resistance is something we looked at in Why Strategies Fail, and we will consider it further when we come to Embedding.

The non-Napoleons, non-entrepreneurs on your committee probably know all about resistance. They may have got where they are by being experts at it. They also know that, with enough organisational resolve, resistance can always be over-come. What they need to decide is, are they willing to give that level of resolve? You don't want to reach a 'back me or sack me' moment,[11] but you do need them to understand that if they

---

11 A friend of mine once tried this ploy when he was marketing director of a London company. The Board immediately took his company car keys off him and had him escorted off the premises. Never risk your strategy on a gesture.

agree to the strategy, they are agreeing to face down whatever internal resistance it produces.

Finally, talk about the Rewards. These are the mixture of tangibles and intangibles that are 'what we really get'. Imagine that your sales really did increase ten-fold. What does that mean? In most businesses it would take you from being a bit-player to one of the top two or three in your market. Or imagine that you are in an NGO and your strategy is to develop a new kind of expertise in disaster management. What would this expertise do for you (and to you)? If it lifted you to the place that you were the go-to organisation for this kind of knowledge for any crisis in the entire world, then the long term impact on your organisation would be dramatic.

Don't oversell this. If your realistic result is an increase in sales of 10%, then talk about what that would mean—for example, going from marginal profitability to full profitability.

Now, you have probably spotted that between getting your strategic idea and the five Rs, there's quite a lot of detail work that needs doing. Remember that STRATEGIST is an iterative process: you are spiralling in on the finished strategy, while at the same time spiralling outwards in terms of how many people you are involving in developing it.

1O minute version

Back to our children lost in the woods. Our strategic insight is that, unless some other, additional, calamity has befallen them, they will eventually find their way onto the road. In one minute, what do we have to do, what's it going to cost, and what are we going to get out of it?

In this case, the people we have to persuade are not a disinterested Board or jaded committee: we have to talk to two sets of worried parents. They will already have run several scenarios through their mind. Risks will be magnified, and the results they are thinking of are deeply disturbing.

Quickly then, what do we need to do? If our insight is correct, we need to send two reliable people—one to drive, one to watch—in a car going round and round the enclosing roads. The *result* is that, within twenty minutes of the boys hitting the road, they will be found by the car. Twenty minutes is long enough for them to realise (if they haven't already) that they are lost, since their goal was in woodland and they are now at the road, but short enough for them not to decide to do something else, such as heading back into the woods to retrace their steps.

The *resources* are two people not prone to panic, and one car. This is only a small proportion of the resources available, and will probably seem disproportionately little to the parents. Hold that thought for a moment.

The *risks* are as follows: first, some other calamity has befallen them. Risk one is that they have perhaps tumbled to the bottom of a cliff and, even if still conscious, are now immobile and will never reach the road. Risk two is they do reach the road, but set off on some other solution of their own before they are found. Risk three is, despite all endeavours, they remain missing after a significant period of time. Risk four is the parents become so worried that they execute their own plan, which gets in the way of the main plan, for example by calling the police too early and putting an end to the search.

How are we to manage these risks? We have people standing around doing nothing, if you recall the Situation section, maps, experienced rescue workers, and some distraught parents. For this, we can turn to the 'obvious' solution, which was to send out search parties. Two search parties in woodland have a relatively low chance of success if the boys are moving, but if the boys are immobilised and either conscious or visible, the chances are better. We can only send out two main parties because without additional experienced leaders, the parties are at risk of falling into trouble themselves.

As far as *resistance* is concerned, this will mainly be from the parents: is the strategy convincing enough? The answer is, yes, but only up to a point. We must have an agreed cut-off at which time we call off the search and call the police. In this case, we decide to allow two hours of searching. Given the size of the woodland, if the boys have not reached the perimeter in three hours (given they were already lost an hour before we started) they are either immobilised or are going round in circles and will never reach it.

What are the *rewards*? As far as the parents are concerned, the principal reward is that pursuing this strategy creates a realistic prospect of the nightmare being over in two hours. If they pursue the alternate strategy of calling the police, they will be forced to wait twenty-four hours before the police will do anything, in which time their ability to search is sharply curtailed. We will consider whether there are any additional rewards later on.

We discuss this briefly with the group, and resolve that we will pursue this strategy.

Two day version

In the two day version, you've now had two sessions of one hour each, which probably means that it's lunch time. After lunch people will return in a benign state of mind, but the blood will have gone to their digestive system, and it is going to be hard work to get them moving again.

In the first afternoon session, you will begin by narrating the idea. Taking what was produced in Situation and Thinking, explain the plan that is beginning to form. It doesn't matter at this stage if it is a particularly good plan, because that is what you are now going to work on. If no idea has come up, instead you can ask the question: "In the light of all this, what should we do?"

Some groups will have got to where you need them in the Thinking session. Other groups need the concrete spur of 'what are we doing to do, and what's that going to achieve' to get their minds into gear. Either way, you do need them to finish this section with a clear idea of what they want to have achieved, generally known as an Outcome, and what kind of approach is going to get them there. In other words, you need an outline of what A is, what B is, and what the route is.

This is why it's a good idea to run this session after lunch. If you've not been making the progress you wanted in the Thinking session, lunch is an opportunity to dig deeper and explore other ideas.

So, as the session begins, you take five minutes to remind them of the situation, and five minutes to encapsulate the idea. That leaves fifty minutes—ten minutes per section—for Results, Resources, Risks, Resistance and Rewards.

For these you can proceed fairly straightforwardly, as discussed above. Don't be afraid to modify and improve the strategic idea as you do this. Discussing these one by one will test the idea. Are the Results actually worth achieving? Some groups will pitch them too low, others will pitch them unfeasibly high.

Are the Resources commensurate with the Results? Remember that 'strategic' means all the resources assigned to achieving all the goals. As well as people, money, equipment and buildings, consider intangible resources like reputation and brand assets. Consider also information resources.

Get them to outline the risks. What is going to happen if you don't do anything, what could go wrong with the plan, what are the risks of success? In most cases these should be fairly obvious. For every step you plan to take, 'it could fail' has to be considered. There is only ten minutes for this section, so work briskly.

When you talk about internal resistance, people tend to clam up. Nobody likes to be known as someone who grumbles about their colleagues. It might help to ask them 'in another organisation, what might the internal resistance be to such a plan?' This is the strategic equivalent of 'asking for a friend'.

If you're running short of time, you can touch lightly on the Rewards. We will pick them up again in the final section, Transformation.

Three month version

If you've spent two weeks each on the first two sections, you are going to need to hurry a little with this one. The lion's share of the work is in identifying the resources you are going to need and in working out what that is going to cost. This is only at the outline level. You will do this in more detail when it comes to Gameplan. If people are stalling (as they often do when it comes to budgets), try to work out what the resource allocation ought to be, based on the scale of the results. If you can promise 'two dollars back for every dollar we put in', then you are doing very well. Most strategies would be accepted if they generate a 10% surplus within manageable risks. Your *results* line must be presented in a SMART format, as above, even if this makes little sense for your strategy.

For *resources*, you need to get your budgeting outline done before you get widespread approval for your strategy. Once the Board has adopted it, and it becomes known that you have significant corporate support, you will discover that things suddenly start to cost a lot more. Instead of being the slightly irritating junior employee who is asking for outline figures for no readily apparent reason, you become the golden boy with the big bankers behind him. People will suddenly look to your strategy as a way of buying things they wanted anyway but couldn't budget for. They may decide to use your interest to justify additional staff. Cherished projects, long mothballed, will be revived and sellotaped to yours.

For *risks*, most large organisations will require you to present a risk register of some kind. Ultimately, a risk register is no more than a collection of opinions about what might happen, but risk managers set great store by them.

A typical risk matrix is shown here:

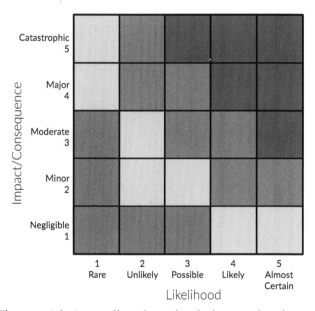

The top right is usually coloured red, the next band orange, the following yellow, and the bottom left green. Anything red would usually be considered an unacceptable threat unless mitigated. Multiplying the Impact and Likelihood scores gives you the overall risk rating, which can be logged in a risk register. A typical format for a risk register might be:

#	Name	Description	Impact	Probability	Rating	Mitigation	Impact after mitigation	Probability after mitigation	Residual risk rating
1	Frogs	Frogs may invade	3	2	6	Close the pond	3	1	3
2	Snakes	Snakes may invade	5	2	10	Put up a sign saying "no snakes"	5	1	5

If you want your strategy to be adopted, you need to show three or four Red risks which, when mitigated by your strategy, are either Green or Yellow. If there are any Red risks after mitigation, the strategy will be rejected. You should not normally list Green risks or Yellow Risks. You might include a couple of Oranges, but these, too, must be mitigated down to Green.

If this sounds like a game, to some extent it is. For most risks you have no way of knowing what the true likelihood is. Nonetheless, as a vocabulary for discussing risks, the Red—Amber—Green ratings, often called 'RAG' ratings, get us a stage further than merely arguing about plausibility.

When it comes to *resistance*, you need to go carefully. You cannot reasonably ask people whether they intend to resist, and those most skilled in doing so won't tell you anyway. See the next section, Allies, for help with this.

Finally, to get the *rewards* right, you need to get your finger on the heartbeat of the organisation. Have lunch with lots of people, and ask them what their deep ambition is. If you frame the Rewards in those terms, the chances of your strategy being accepted, and, more importantly, being the right strategy, increase.

4 Allies

The Political school of strategy sees the strategic process as a series of negotiations. It follows naturally from Resolve, because it is when you publicly articulate your plans that people and groups start lining up for you, or against you.

You might imagine that simply outlining a programme of public good will be enough to make everyone like you. The reality is somewhat different.

Some will support you even though they don't agree with you, because they see a reputational value in public support. However, they may be less forthcoming when it comes to actual help.

Some will oppose you even though they do agree with you, because they see your programme as competition for their's, or a boost in your reputation as equivalent to a dent for them.

Some will support your programme because of spin-off benefits. Some will oppose it because of negative side-effects, real or imagined.

Strategic question 4: Who is with us?

Good allies—the ones which genuinely agree with your strategy, and have something to contribute—bring four things. First, they may bring enhanced resources. Second, they may bring particular skills, knowledge or tactics. Third, they bring reputation. Fourth, they connect you to other potential allies.

At the same time, allies also come at a cost. They may expect you to support their programmes in return. They may expect to be on a steering committee which will dilute the strategy. They may put off other potential allies. They may consume more time in managing the alliance than they contribute.

Enemies are sometimes more useful than allies. If you are trying to get publicity, a good enemy can keep your project in the newspapers, on broadcasts, and on social media for months. They can shore up support for what you're doing, and cause waverers to commit. If you are trying to get elected to a committee—remember that this school of strategy was designed around politics—you only need to get 51% of the available vote in order to win. It doesn't actually matter if the other 49% of voters are your sworn enemies, at least, not during the election, though you may come to need them later. Many would-be politicians discover the dangers of being liked by everyone, but not loved by anyone: in a first-past-the-post system, being everyone's second choice gets you exactly nowhere. In that case, it can be better to engender strong reactions. Your enemies can help to cement your alliances.

If this seems rather cold and calculating, it's worth remembering that thinking in a political way does not require you to act unethically. Indeed, many politicians in later life regret the unethical actions of their youth, which come back to haunt them. Acting ethically often has a short term cost for the politician—loss of promised support, be it votes, funding or recommendation. However, acting unethically has a recurrent cost which only grows over time.

Many people shy away from the political, but it affects all strategies. Those who avoid thinking about it are easily outman-oeuvred by internal resistors and overwhelmed by external pressure. You do not need to engage in political or quasi-political activity, but you do need to understand the network of relationships which affect your strategy.

The most widely used method of looking at this is the Stakeholder Analysis, as in the diagram below, but, this is not as useful as it might appear. The underlying notion is that groups with high influence and high interest should be managed closely, those with high interest but low influence should be kept informed, those with high influence but low interest should be kept satisfied, and those with low interest and low influence should just be monitored.

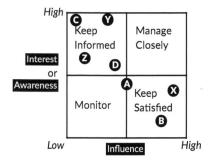

Stakeholder analysis

A common way of considering the political aspects of strategy is with a stakeholder analysis, where you place different players by their interest/awareness and influence. However, if slavishly followed, this can lead to some unhelpful results. See the next diagram for why.

If you are working with a long list of stakeholders, and want to know who you should be paying attention to, this can be helpful. However, what it doesn't recognise is that your stakeholders talk to each other, and they are not all benign. If you are, for example, consulting on changes to a hospital service, a user group may be 'high in interest' but 'low in influence'. However, if they start writing letters to their local Member of Parliament (to give a UK example), who may, up to that point, have been low in interest, you may suddenly find yourself with a problem.

We prefer the network diagram, below, which maps out who listens to whom. This is not about general influence, but about specific influence. It highlights the danger which the stakeholder diagram misses. If X is the local Member of Parliament, who you relate to directly, and Y and Z are user groups hostile to the changes you want to bring about, there is a significant danger that they Y and Z will pull the parliamentarian into direct opposition. A, B, C and D are a bit more complicated. A and B talk to D, and they talk to each other, and they talk to C. If you can draw D into your allies circle, then this is probably enough to keep A neutral, and might even lead B to become neutral rather than remaining hostile. If you do nothing, there is a good chance that C will will draw A into outright opposition.

Diagrams of this type are just tools: they can help you spot dangers and opportunities that you would otherwise have missed. However, ultimately, you are drawing a picture of your own opinion. If your opinions, or those of the people you listen to, are poorly informed, then your diagram will be as well.

Whatever diagram you use, make sure you don't leave it lying around. Stakeholders do not take kindly to discovering a piece of paper that marks them as 'low influence', or as 'enemies'.

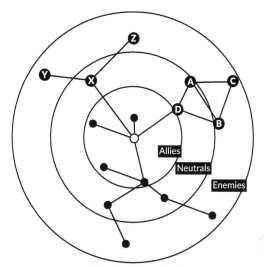

Mapping the network

In this diagram, you are mapping the relationships between different players, and roughly categorising them as allies, neutrals or enemies. Players are likely to line up with their friends. You are the white dot in the middle. All other things being equal, Neutral X is likely to be pulled into active opposition by Y and Z. C is pulling on A and B, with A just in the neutral zone and B in active opposition. However, if you can help D move from benign neutrality to actively supporting you, this could keep A safely neutral, and B might move from opposition to neutrality.

1O minute version

At the ten minute level, you do not have time to get involved in complicated mapping. You simply need to jot down two lists, each with two columns. The first is 'Allies' with 'What can they do?' and the second is 'Opponents' with 'What might they do?'

Let's go back to the lost children. In one minute, we learn the following:

Allies	*What can they do?*
Reliable driver & friend	Drive round the roads
Experienced rescue workers	Lead search parties
Team members	Take part in search parties
Parents	Probably not much (too emotionally involved)

Opponents	*What might they do?*
Local Police	Stop the search for 24 hours

Now, in this case, note that the opponents include the local police. They have no malicious intent, but their protocol says that they need to wait 24 hours before launching a search. If we reach the two hour cut-off point, we change the strategy, and at that point they become our key allies. They are not necessarily against us doing our own searching right now, but, by protocol, they must put a stop to the strategy once formally involved.

This is a good example of how the Resolve changes who the allies and opponents are. If the Resolve is to involve the police as soon as possible, then the Opponents in the existing strategy become Allies, and the existing Allies end up with little to do.

Two day version

A one hour session is a good opportunity to do the network map we looked at on the previous page. You will need to do it in three parts.

First, get the group to brainstorm who has an influence on your programme. Make a list. You can push them to be creative on this. Take a quarter of an hour.

Second, get them to map out 'who listens to who', in circles of allies, neutrals and enemies. You may need to sketch this a couple of times, and don't be scared of crossing things out, moving them around and generally playing with it until it reflects the understanding in the room. Your circles don't need to be circular! Take twenty minutes on this.

Third, for each of the players that are perceived to be likely opponents, get the group to answer the question 'why?'

Let's take another real life example. You have two hospitals. One is medium-sized, in the centre of the town, with good access to road, rail and bus, average facilities, and a complete complement of doctors and nurses. The other is tiny, out in the countryside, has only one infrequent bus service, is decades out of date, no on-site doctors and a minimum number of nurses. It's mainly used for 'rehabilitation', but recent investigations show that it has a poor track record. It's obvious that you need to close it, and invest the money in upgrading the care in the main hospital.

However, before your Board has even got as far as discussing it, the whole thing gets leaked to the newspapers. A campaign group is formed. From nowhere a petition with 16,000 signatures appears. Local politicians speak out against you, TV, newspapers and radio run the story as 'save our hospital', and internal stakeholders are in danger of losing their nerve.

Let's imagine that you do the exercise as discussed above. Each stage should produce some new information, which one person in the group might already know, but is not part of the shared knowledge.

First, in the listing phase, you learn that the campaign group is headed by some local ex-councillors who lost their seats in something vaguely scandalous a few years before, and are now standing to be re-elected.

Second, in the mapping phase, you discover that they are closely linked with a union representative who gets the confidential Board papers. You probably don't need to look much further for your leak, but you probably also need to find a way to plug it.

Third, the 'Why?' phase throws up some other information. It turns out that some people worried that the land on which the hospital is built will be sold off for housing. If you're not from the UK, this might surprise you as an issue, but people do get very worried when assets of the health service are sold to private buyers. Some people are worried that, when they need rehabilitation, there won't be any. The ex-councillors see it as an opportunity for re-election. The newspapers, TV and radio are just after a good, newsworthy story, and 'save our hospital' is usually a story that gets public attention. The union rep is worried that the hospital nurses will lose their jobs.

Three month version

In the three month version, give yourself one week to sound out the various groups you identified in the two day workshop. What are the possibilities of moving neutrals into the allies camp, and opponents into the neutrals camp? There is often more to be gained than you might think.

There are four things you can do as you sound out these groups. In increasing order of cost, they are:

1 Contact
2 Information
3 Explanation
4 Negotiation.

Simply making **contact** can do a lot to alleviate suspicions. A phone conversation or face-to-face meeting which you initiate has many benefits.

Information is more expensive. In our hospital example, any information issued is going to be used time and again during the consultation process. On the one hand, groups want the information now, on the other, they want it to be something they can rely on. This is the old struggle between 'do it right' and 'do it now'.

Explanation, in the sense of answering their questions, is more costly than information, and more risky. When asked questions to which we don't know the answer, most of us try to explain, but if our explanations are not the real explanations, or represent only a part of the picture, people will feel cheated when they eventually discover what is actually going on. Fake explanations are one of the fastest ways to push people into firm opposition.

Negotiation is the most costly, and it may not be possible to negotiate with every group. In our example, the nurses who are afraid of losing their jobs could probably benefit from some kind of negotiated deal. Newspapers, TV and radio will not negotiate, though they will probably agree to present a balanced response if you are willing to give one. Any attempt to negotiate with the people trying to use the protest to get themselves re-elected is likely to backfire.

Being aware of the politics doesn't mean you have to back down if you can't get support. Sometimes it's a question of holding your nerve. Groups that vocally oppose what you are doing seldom have the power to stop you. Understanding who really does have the power to shut you down, though, is crucial: otherwise you may discover that someone you did not know existed has listened to someone you discounted, and your strategy is over before it has started.

5 Tactics

 Tactics comes after Allies, because your allies bring with them tactics that you would not otherwise have access to.

What is a tactic, and what is the tactical, or Positioning school of strategy? Essentially a tactic is a repeatable combination of actions that you can deploy as a unit. 'Buy low, sell high' is a tactic, because it combines two distinct actions.

The Positioning school of strategy[12] is about taking up particular positions which are often in the form of 'in situation x, do y'. The most famous text in this school is Sun Tzu's The Art of War, an early Chinese treatise on military strategy. It contains gems such as 'know your enemy and know yourself, and in a thousand battles you will not be defeated' and 'ultimate excellence lies not in winning a thousand fights, but in winning without ever fighting'. Advocates of the Positioning school

---

12 People who talk about 'The Art of War' by Sun Tzu, or 'On War' by Clauswicz, or Game Theory are usually from the Positioning school, even if they aren't aware of the term.

suggest that the sum total of strategy is a series of applicable maxims which can be used to guide the organisation without necessarily adopting any particular pre-planned course of action.

People easily get confused between the ideas of strategy and tactics. One way of putting the distinction is to say that strategy is about winning the whole war, whereas tactics is about winning the individual battle. However, outside of the military arena, these explanations can cloud as much as they clarify.

Strategic question 5: What are we good at?

At the heart of tactics is that they are communicable, teachable, practiceable, repeatable and deliberate.

Communicable: you should be able to name a tactic and ask for it to be deployed without having to explain it again.

Teachable: in most cases, tactics are not 'obvious'. One tactic in driving is 'Mirror, Signal, Manoeuvre'. A learner driver is unlikely to guess that for themselves, but they can be taught it quite easily by an instructor.

Practiceable: most tactics work better if they are practised and can be executed without thinking.

Repeatable: to be a tactic, you must be able to deploy it as often as you want.

Deliberate: you need to be able to deploy a tactic when you choose to, but also refrain. A tactic is not simply a learned behaviour.

In the sport of fencing, two basic actions are the step forward and the lunge. Beginners practice them individually, but advanced fencers practice them in combination. Tactically speaking, they can be combined as a slow step and a fast lunge, a fast step and a slow lunge, a fast step and fast lunge, and a slow step and slow lunge. The most generally productive is the slow step fast lunge, because most opposing fencers respond to the speed of the slow step, and are surprised when it develops into a fast lunge. However, the effectiveness wears off once the other fencer spots what you are doing. Mixing the four tactics keeps the other fencer confused. This mixing itself becomes a tactic in its own right: it's a good example of how you can combine simple tactics into more complex ones.

The Tactical or Positioning school of strategy is not to everyone's taste. The idea of having 'tactics' suggests we are treating what we are doing like a game, or like a fight. If you are trying to organise a charity concert, or book a holiday, the notion of tactics may seem out of place, especially if you associate the word 'tactic' with 'trickery'.

Another way of seeing it is by asking the question 'what are we good at?' In the case of a concert, you might use a free online ticket sales service. This tactic takes pressure off you, and broadens your scope. You've in fact co-opted an ally to make this tactic available. Once you've done this for one concert, you can keep doing it for others.

If you're booking a holiday, a tactic might be to use a flight booking website which continually updates prices. This will give you the best deal today, but you can get an even better deal if you start early and check the website daily. You'll discover that there are cheaper and more expensive days to buy tickets (as it happens, Tuesday is the cheapest day on which to purchase most tickets, and Saturday the most expensive). Although you're co-opting a website as a tactic, you're combining it with the tactic of comparing over time to create a more advanced, more effective tactic.

1O minute version

In a single minute, you have time to identify what tactics your various allies bring to the table.

In the missing children example, we've got one person who has been trained in emergencies, and someone else with wilderness experience, so the tactic they make available is leading a search party. Driving round the road loop is also a tactic, and we recognise that it has to be done repeatedly to be effective. Once is almost certainly not enough.

There are lots of other tactics available, but the strategic skill we're developing is spotting which of them fit with the strategic idea we came up with in the Thinking section, and decided on in the Resolve section. Good tactics can also be a matter of stopping doing the obvious things. In this case, the obvious tactic is to put everyone onto search teams, but these have (in our strategic idea) a much lower chance of success than driving the loop. What's more, unless we deliberately organise people, they will set off on impromptu search teams of their own, on the (all too common) reasoning of 'something must be done, this is something, therefore this must be done'. Without additional skilled people to lead search teams, they are as likely to get themselves into trouble as do any good.

Another adage worth remembering is 'to a hammer, everything looks like a nail'. If the team has a particular tactic they are good at, they will tend to employ it even when it's inappropriate.

Therefore, in a minute, decide what tactics are available that should be used, and which 'obvious' tactics should be held back.

Two day version

In a one hour session, you have time to brainstorm four categories:

- What tactics to do we have (ie, what are we good at)?
- What tactics do our allies have (ie, what are they known for)?
- What tactics have we seen or heard about that we might try?
- What new tactics should we develop to make our idea work?

Spend ten minutes introducing the idea of tactics, and then ten minutes on each of these. That leaves you ten minutes at the end. Use this to ask: 'are there ways we can combine tactics into new things that are more powerful?'

For example, if you are putting on a charity concert, chances are that you have some musicians. An obvious tactic organising a concert is to hand out flyers, but supposing you had two people handing out flyers, and one playing the trumpet while they do it. Supposing that the flyers have a picture of a trumpet on them? Or, suppose that you had the flyers printed in the shape of a trumpet. You could potentially get flyers printed in different shapes, and have different musicians accompanying the appropriate shape of flyer.

Three month version

If you take a week to work on tactics, you have a chance to go and interview the people you can involve. Most people struggle to distinguish between strategy and tactics, or, more exactly, when asked for a strategy, they merely offer a list of tactics. Very few people will thank you for lecturing them on this subject, but if you go to see them and explain the problem and the strategic idea (you can call it 'the approach' if that helps), and ask them how they would tackle it, you will usually get a good picture of the kinds of tactics they can contribute.

Generally speaking, the broader the range of tactics, the more creatively you can combine them. If you are working in a large organisation, take time to talk to the people who usually don't get asked. Hospital porters and the guys who work in the mail room can often solve a tricky logistical problem that their managers would struggle to understand. In many cases, you'll find that these people proposed the solution to your problem years before, but nobody listened to them. Applying their insights—and giving them credit for it—can help develop powerful allies who will consistently come to your rescue when the implementation of the programme begins to get sticky: and it will always get sticky at some point.

As a general rule, the more ignored, despised or sidelined people are, the more chance that they have things to contribute which nobody knows about. Combining tactics from different parts of the organisation and from allies will frequently produce powerful solutions which have never been tried anywhere else. There may be other spin-off benefits.

6 Embedding

Here we look at embedding the strategy. The Cultural school to strategy is that success flows from strong culture. It grew strongly during the 1970s and 1980s when Japanese and later South Korean companies began to win American and European markets with products which were better designed, better engineered and more consistently manufactured than established Western brands[13]. This led to a series of cultural change programmes, of which the best known is probably Total Quality Management (TQM). Rather than focussing on big bosses with big ideas (the Entrepreneurial school) or ever more scientific resource management, cultural approaches focus on improving morale, fostering innovation at the individual level, and creating a strong shared identity.

We agree that culture can make or break strategy. Your organisation's culture will make it more or less receptive to new ideas,

---

13 The phrase 'Culture eats strategy for breakfast' is usually attributed to Peter Drucker, though it was popularised by Mark Fields of Ford.

will determine what things are accepted and what are resisted, and will foster communication or miscommunication.

At the same time, we think that most of the widely used methods of setting organisational culture are doomed.

Most organisations we've looked at that are trying to change their culture focus on things like mission statements, vision statements and declared values.

We'll come back to why we think these aren't effective in a moment, but it's worth first thinking about what organisational culture is.

Great cultures are shaped by their darkest moments. Londoners still talk about the 'Blitz spirit'. Part of the drive at Apple comes from the fact that it almost went out of business before Steve Jobs returned to bring it back from the near-dead. Lynyrd Skynyrd is still touring forty-nine years after it chose its name, not so much 'despite of' but 'because of' the 1977 air crash which killed three of its members.

However, even organisations which are new and have had no dark moments have culture.

Culture is communicated by shared stories, shared rituals and shared language. In a strong culture, people start to dress like each other, tell the same jokes and even listen to the same music.

But this, too, is how culture is expressed, not what it is.

Strategic question 6: What are we doing that's different, and how will we take people with us?

Fundamentally, if your strategy doesn't go against your culture in terms of what you intend to do, then it isn't a strategy, it's just 'doing what we always do'. But if you do want to do something new, you also to have harness organisational culture to get you there.

At the base, culture depends on world-view. World-view is a set of assumptions we make about the world around us, or, put another way, the filters and perspectives we use to cope with our experience of life.

Classically, this falls into three categories: ontology, epistemology, and deontology. Ontology is our beliefs about what exists, and how it is categorised. Epistemology is how we know what we know, or how we decide what truth is. Deontology is how we reason about right and wrong.

When it comes to defining and changing culture, most organisations work in the area of ontology. This is what mission statements and vision statements do—they define what the business of the organisation is (what is) and how they want things to be in the future (what will be). Their reward systems are usually based on money (a thing) or on status, or on the prospects of promotion and career longevity.

In contemporary culture, law prescribes what organisations are allowed to do, and money determines if the people who work there are willing to do it. In a typical commercial company, staff are prepared to work extra hours, as long as they're paid overtime. Managers are willing to work longer in return for the prospect of promotion: they are effectively trading time now for substantially better pay in the future. Nonetheless, one of the lessons of two generations of failed attempts to change culture in Western manufacturing is that you can't buy it.

Culture change is almost always gradual, even in dark hours, but it is not random. When strategy is put forward, people respond to it based on their underlying epistemology and deontology far more than on their ontology.

Let's take these two separately.

For **epistemology** (how we know), different people have different views about what makes for believable information, and what makes promises about the future credible, which is what a strategy is. Strong organisational cultures, which are the hardest to change, tend to have a shared epistemology.

Depending on the person and the culture, one or more of these will be considered more trustworthy:

- What is said   (we trust people who say things)
- What is observed   (we make up our own minds)
- What is experienced (we believe what we've taken part in)
- What is taught   (we believe authoritative information)
- What is measured   (we believe data)
- What is reasoned   (we believe what is plausible).

In a '**said**' culture, if the chief executive or other organisational leader puts her or his reputation on the line, the staff or volunteers will usually align with the strategy.

In an '**observed**' culture, it is largely irrelevant what organisational leaders say, until the team observes them acting in a new way. Inconsistency, or perceived inconsistency, will mean the end of it.

To win people over in an '**experienced**' culture, they need to take part, often in a role-play, pilot programme or exercise. Sports clubs are often 'experienced' cultures. A new coach coming in needs to demonstrate an improved sporting experience before being accepted.

In a '**taught**' culture, great store is set by what was learned in formal courses, or is published in reputable journals, or stated by acknowledged experts.

In a '**measured**' culture, data is king. The data needs to be unambiguous, because people who care a lot about data are usually skilled in interpreting it.

In a '**reasoned**' culture, only 'what makes sense' is accepted. This does not necessarily mean it must be logically compelling. Reasoned cultures accept the plausible intuitively. Logic is one way of triggering this intuition, but so are analogies, narratives and other ways of appealing to the rational sense.

In the 21st century, it's been proposed that there are three kinds of worldview[14], which are **honour-shame, innocence-guilt** and **power-fear**. Though we think that this is overselling the concept, because it doesn't cover ontological and epistemological aspects of worldview, it is clearly a valuable tool for understanding **deontic worldview: what 'ought'**.

In a **power-fear** culture, we 'ought' to obey authorities, whether we agree with them or understand their moral reasoning or not. Hierarchical strata are strictly maintained, and ranks are clearly delineated, as they must be, otherwise we don't know who we should obey. Written rules are treated as proxies for the authorities which issued them. Interpreting them is about interpreting the intention behind the rules.

In an **honour-shame** culture, we 'ought' to do things which bring honour to those it is honourable for us to honour. This might mean acting in a way which brings honour to our parents, to our school, to our company or to our regiment. Written rules are interpreted on the basis that they are made with honour in mind, which means that a rule might be discounted in a particular situation if it would be dishonourable to obey it. For example, a commanding officer might lie to the police in order to protect a fighter pilot on active duty.

Recent thinking suggests that power-fear is a subculture within honour-shame culture.

In an **innocence-guilt** culture, what is 'objectively' right coincides with our conscience. If written rules disagree, the written rules are wrong. Doing what is dishonest or immoral puts us into a state of guilt. Right and wrong have an objective meaning, irrespective of the power or status of those involved. When dealing with written rules, the exact text is normative, not

---

14 First by Roland Muller in Muller, Roland. (2000). Honor and shame: Unlocking the door. United States: XLibris Corporation

the supposed 'intention'. This prompts public discussion about the rules, something strictly avoided in honour-shame and power-fear cultures.

Even within a national culture which is predominantly one thing, an organisation, or a functional unit within an organisation, may have its own sub-culture. Appealing to the wrong kind of deontic, moral, reasoning can backfire. You will also notice that situations can change approach. In a crisis, some people may be much more inclined to follow orders, while others may suddenly want to agonise about right and wrong.

If you are proposing a change in strategy, you might do so in one of three ways:

"We are doing it because it is right,"

"We are doing it because it is honourable,"

"We are doing it because the boss says we should."

All these are 'we are doing it because we must', but 'must' means different things. To someone from an innocence-guilt background, 'do what you're told' can prompt strong moral indignation. On the other hand, to someone from a power-fear culture, the kind of moral reasoning that an innocence-guilt person wants to engage in looks like some kind of duplicity: a trick to argue that white is black and black is white.

Navigating culture is difficult enough. Changing culture even more so. You would be unwise to try to change deontic or epistemological culture. There is very rarely any benefit in doing so, and it runs too deep to be amenable to deliberate change. However, in changing ontological culture—what we are for, we what we do, what we want to achieve—you can achieve success by understanding and appealing to how people perceive truth, and how they perceive right and wrong.

We mentioned earlier that cultural change programmes that focus on mission and vision statements and declared values rarely work. Mission statements are really the province of mission organisations: either Christian missions, or diplomatic missions, or military missions. Their fundamental characteristic is that they are sent out and may no longer have regular contact with those that sent them (this was more true of the days before telephone, and internet). The mission statement is a guiding principle when contact with the headquarters is limited. If HQ is regularly in touch with all its departments, and isn't willing to relinquish decision-making to a lower level, then a mission statement is just decoration.

Declared values are a slightly different matter. Most organisations that have them have a subset of the same handful: passion, integrity, team-work, and so on.

If you want an effective and realistic set of values to work with, then begin with the behaviours you want to change. Start by saying "we hate it when..." Then reverse it. "We love it when..." Reduce that down to single words, and you have a list of values which are the things you would rather abandon a programme rather than compromise. They will be unique to your organisation, and your staff team will recognise their appropriateness and importance.

10 minute version

In a single minute, you can ask yourself two questions: first, is the culture a good ontological fit for the strategic idea? If yes, you can immediately proceed to outlining what you intend. For example, you are in an organisation with a strong bias toward action and daring, and you want to propose something which is active and daring. In doing so, you might want to check yourself: has the culture actually overridden your strategic sense? If you are just doing what your organisational culture requires, are you in fact doing strategy at all, or merely doing the 'obvious' thing?

If no, then you need to ask yourself: what will convince people of the truth of the situation (epistemology), and what will convince them of the moral imperative behind the idea (deontology)?

In our lost children example, the group culture is biased toward action. It is very easy to send out search parties, comparatively harder to take the 'easy' route of having a car drive round and round the road loop. Helpfully for us, we can count on rich information to cover most of the 'how do I know this is true' issues. Because everyone involved is at the venue, they have observed, are experiencing and are hearing exactly the same things. Those who have been taught crisis management will recognise the need to follow a chain of command, even if this is not their natural approach, and those who like measurement will appreciate that we are 'on the clock', with a decision to call the police at 17:30 rather than a vaguer decision to 'carry on until it's late' helping them to accept the strategic idea.

Is it necessary to explain the strategic idea, that the children will most likely make their way to the road? Actually, no. Explanation can appear to be an invitation to debate, and, in this particular situation, there is no time for debate.

Two day version

In a one hour session, there is probably not enough time to do full justice to ontology, epistemology and deontology, but there is more than enough time to ask the right questions.

The first question, which you can take fifteen minutes for, is 'how is what we are proposing different from what we usually do?' If the answer is 'it's what we always do', then it may be best to review the strategic idea. Better to understand here that we are merely going with our default answer than to pursue it without considering alternatives. If the answer is 'no, this is different', spend the rest of the fifteen minutes identifying what is different, and what is therefore likely to cause resistance.

Take twenty minutes for the next question: what is persuasive to people in our organisation? You can give a couple of examples—some people believe what they hear from the boss, some people believe data—but don't give all the examples, because you want your team to figure it out for themselves. This will lead to a richer, more productive conversation, because you are not interested in what they *generally* find convincing, but what they are going to specifically find convincing in your project.

This is where your colleagues will start pointing to issues in the past which have made some things more or less credible. For example, if you are in a culture such as a hospital which is normally heavily reliant on data as evidence, someone may highlight an occasion when everyone relied on the data, but the data was later shown to be faulty. This might draw a line between, for example, measurements of patient conditions by nurses, and aggregated financial data based on late night coding by emergency room administrators. The result could therefore be that staff generally believed measured data, but when it comes to financial data they insist on supplementing it with observation, experience or an authoritative source.

If the conversation seems to be catching fire, you can let it run on a little, and then throw in the question about how people feel morally about change, and how they are likely to feel about the specific strategic idea. People in the room may want to voice their own moral qualms at this point, and you must give them the freedom to do so. If no one raises any objections of their own, put the question in a different way: "if you were asking for a friend, what kind of moral questions do you think this strategic idea might raise?" Most people will find it easier to pinpoint what is morally persuasive if they are thinking of a specific objection.

The culture session, about how you embed strategy into the organisation, is the sixth. You can either run this at the end of the first day, which gives you scope to let the conversation run on past the hour, or you can start the second day with it. This depends a little on how exhausted people are after the first five sessions.

To wrap it up, sketch out this diagram on a whiteboard:

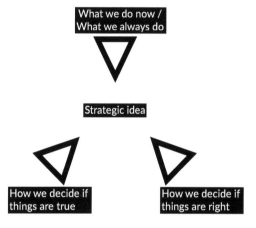

Write in what we always do, how we know if things are true and how we decide if things are right, as well as the strategic idea, in place of the labels used here. Do a sanity check: is the strategic idea different from what we always do? If it isn't, then it isn't a strategy, it's just a continuation. At the bottom, you should now have a list of what you have to do in order to make the case for the new strategy. People will buy into almost any strategy if they think that the situation warrants it, the strategy is credible and it is right. They won't buy into it if you have not satisfied their requirements for truth and morality.

Three month version

Working on a three month planning cycle, you have time not only to discover culture, using the method above, but also to take some steps.

It may be that what you need to do is organise a communication campaign to let everyone know what is happening, providing each cultural group (including among your allies, who may have very different cultures) with arguments they will believe and morally support.

However, this is not always enough. It may be that your strategic idea, in its current form, is not credible or not morally acceptable to some of the people you need on board.

To return to an earlier example, when we were closing down an unnecessary (and, frankly, dangerous) hospital, we learned through discussions that many of the staff had real moral concerns about selling off health service property for housing. They felt that the land had was somehow held in trust for the general good, and should not simply be sold off to a profit-making concern.

We looked at these issues, and decided to broker funding for a hospice to be built on the site. For the staff who had concerns, this was compelling. When we talked to members of the public, some of them said that they would only believe it when they saw the hospice being built: they agreed morally that it was a good idea, but they stood by 'seeing is believing'.

We then rang up the leader of the campaign group. He listened to our plans, and said that he thought a hospice would be very good for the borough. But then he said "we'll still oppose it." He was working from a power-fear basis where ceding power in the situation was not something he would accept. From his perspective, it was more important to be re-elected to the local authority—which he thought he would get by leading opposition to the closure—than to accept the inter-mediate victory of preventing the land being sold off for hous-ing. From his moral perspective, he was acting uprightly and rationally.

As it happened in that situation, it was enough for us to win over the hospital staff. They were the true stakeholders.

In this case, understanding the culture of the health service (and being part of it ourselves), we were able to recognise that closing the hospital and selling off the land in one go would be perceived as a breach of trust. This was not something that could be rationally analysed from an innocence-guilt point of view. It was an honour-shame understanding. In fact, we did eventually commission an outside body, a hospice charity, to run the hospice, but this, from the point of view of our stakeholders, was fundamentally different from selling off the land for a commercial purpose.

In other words, we recognised that the strategy needed an additional element to be culturally viable.

As it happens, this also lifted the strategy from being no more than doing what we would naturally do (though, in fact, our predecessors should have done the job, but lacked the resolve) to something far more significant. The borough had been miss-ing a hospice for more than twenty years, and was no closer to acquiring one. We also commissioned a whole raft of intermedi-ate care services to meet the needs the hospital should have been fulfilling but wasn't.

Culture is in some ways like a strong wind. Sometimes you can harness it, by building turbines, sometimes you can with-stand it, but sometimes you have to bend around it. The trick, as they say, is in knowing which.

7 Gameplan

For many people, a strategy is a plan. It runs in a linear fashion from beginning to end. If strategy is getting from A to B in a better way, it is simply a matter of working out the best route, breaking it down into steps, and then following it.

Now, we hope that we've already made the case that there is more to strategy than a simple plan. Nonetheless, most strategies will involve a plan of some kind.

The Planning school of strategy was the great innovation of the twentieth century, as far as business was concerned, though in military terms it it goes all the way back to Napoleon.

Scientific planning allows you to project a major programme into the future. Working backwards from the end (a key innovation of the Planning school), you follow the chain of 'because of', back to the situation at the start. In doing so, you identify the resources you will need, when they have to be ready, what it will cost, and what are the critical items (known as a critical path) that delay the whole project if they overrun.

If you've been brought up in the Planning school—it is by far the most widely taught method—you may be thinking at this point that such a plan is all you need, and the preceding (and following) sections are unnecessary padding.

This is incorrect.

Plans of this kind are fine for simple and complicated situations, but run into trouble when you come into complex and chaotic situations[15]. 'Simple' is straightforward cause followed by effect, and 'complicated' is a series of simple actions built up into a more intricate pattern. 'Complex', by contrast, is where you have multiple contributory factors, some of which are outside your control. 'Chaotic' is when the factors are not only outside your control, but also outside your understanding.

A good example of this is the competing military strategies at the start of the First World War. This was perhaps best analysed by Barbara W Tuchman in her seminal book The Guns of August[16], but, in highly simplified form, it boils down to the fact that the German Schlieffen Plan and the French Plan XVII were both derived from the experiences of the Franco-Prussian war, 1870. Both sides saw the key to military victory in outflanking the other. Either plan could have worked, but in combination the logical, inevitable, result was that the two armies spread themselves out into thin lines that ran from the coast at one end to the mountains at the other. These lines quickly coalesced into the horrors of trench warfare, in which millions lost their lives.

A plan is good for building a house, or a tunnel, or organising a concert, but poor when the situation is changing.

15 This formulation was first seen in A Leader's Framework for Decision Making, David J Snowden and Mary E Boone, Harvard Business Review, November 2007.

16 The Guns of August, Barbara W Tuchman, Macmillan 1962.

Strategic question 7: What steps must we take, and in what order?

The elements of a good plan are as follows:

First, it should be an **unbroken chain of cause and effect**. You can (and will) add additional causes at various points in the plan, but nothing in the plan should result from anything but the situation at the beginning, and the steps taken previously in the plan. A plan can contain contingencies for when things go wrong, but it must not rely on things going unexpectedly right.

Second, the plan proceeds through a series of steps which are sets of **actions culminating in the achievement of intermediate goals**. These goals must be Specific, Measurable, Achievable, Realistic and Timed (SMART).

Third, these **steps depend on each other**. Known as 'dependencies', these are most often 'finish to start', which is to say the next step depends on the previous one finishing in order to start, but can also be 'start to start', so that two steps begin at the same time, 'finish to finish', which is when they must finish together, or, potentially but unusually, 'start to finish', which is really a 'finish to start'.

Fourth, the steps are calculated **from end to beginning**. In some senses they resemble a river, with all the different tributaries coming together at or before the final goal.

One of the great advantages of project planning is that it can be fully automated using a computer. Many project planning applications exist, of which the best known is Microsoft Project. However, project planning methodology was established long before computers were generally available. You can sketch out a plan on an envelope without any access to a computer.

There are three widely used project planning tools: PERT diagrams, Gantt charts and Critical Path Management (CPM).

Gantt charts are the easiest to grasp. Essentially, you sketch out a chart of days, weeks, months or even years, depending on the project scale, and then you draw a horizontal bar for each step in the project, running from the planned start of the step until the planned finish. You can draw thin lines between to connect them up, showing the dependencies.

Gantt charts give an easily understood picture of the steps.

If your plan has more than a few steps, but you aren't ready to move to project planning software, you can use a spreadsheet showing the start date, estimated duration, finish date, required resources and dependencies. A simple formula will allow the start to be calculated from the finish based on estimated duration.

ID	Name	Start	Finish	Duration	Resources	Depends on
1	Place bed order	01-Oct	01-Oct	1h	Mike	
2	Bed delivery	07-Oct	07-Oct	1d	Mike	1
3	Assemble bed	09-Oct	09-Oct	4h	Mike, Jenn	2
4	Order paint	05-Oct	05-Oct	1h	Jenn	
5	Collect paint	07-Oct	07-Oct	1h	Jenn	4
6	Paint bed	08-Oct	08-Oct	4h	Mike, Jenn	3,5
7	Allow to dry	09-Oct	11-Oct	3d		6
8	Touch up	12-Oct	12-Oct	2h	Jenn	7

You would usually map out a plan at various scales. A common way to think about this is the 'world atlas' level, the 'regional map' level, and the 'street by street' level. The 'world atlas' level can be easily mapped out in a few steps by sketching Gantt charts. The next level, which might have fifty or a hundred steps, is better done using some kind of simple computer list, such as the Excel spreadsheet we just mentioned.

Be wary of buying advanced computer project software. If you can't manage a project by sketching it out, you won't do any better in software, but you will tie yourself in knots trying to fill in all of the information the software asks you for. Most computer-based project plans are never finished, and they're never consulted once they are finished.

A project plan is a tool for managing the project. If you are using a plan, you need to be regularly checking that it is on course, and regularly updating it as the project progresses.

An alternative way to plan a project is as a flow chart. This is the basis of PERT diagrams, though PERT is a methodology with more elements. If you want to look into PERT, any book about project management will explain it. For non-specialist planners, a simple chart of boxes linked together with arrows helps to understand what has to happen for other things to happen.

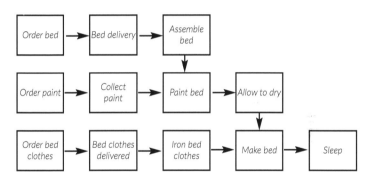

The trick to all planning is to work from the end goal. In the example above, in order to sleep, you must make the bed. In order to make the bed, you must have ironed the bed clothes, and the paint must have dried. In order for the paint to dry, it must be painted, and in order for that to happen, it must be assembled and the paint must be delivered. And so on.

You might not come up with that project plan straight away. Your high level plan might be: Order bed, Make bed, Sleep. It's when you look at the bed you want to order that you discover that it arrives unassembled, and unpainted, and when you think about newly purchased bed clothes that you realise they are always a bit itchy until they've been ironed.

So, three adages for planners:

* Know your end goal
* Know your resources
* Know who is going to do what.

Another way of looking at this is to say, 'check your standard questions for everything', the standard questions being: Who? What? When? Where? How? Why?

We saw earlier that planning systems are good for the complicated. For simple projects, a list will suffice.

A simple project could be boiling an egg: heat the water, put the egg in, let it boil for three minutes, remove the egg, serve in an egg cup. In this case, every item follows one preceding item, and there are no options as to order.

A complicated project might be making lasagne. To do so, you need to prepare the roux sauce at the same time that you are preparing the Bolognese sauce, and you must have pre-heated the oven by the time you put the lasagne into it. There's an additional process of layering pasta. To successfully make lasagne, you need to begin each process at the right time and manage their speed so that the layers of pasta and Bolognese are ready to be topped off with the roux when the oven is pre-heated, forty-five minutes before you want to serve it.

This is where planning reaches the end of its usefulness. Let's imagine that you arrive at a party near where you live, and discover the power is out. All the food has been prepared, but it will start to cool down pretty quickly, as it was supposed to be kept on food heaters. A call to the property owner tells you that the power won't be on until tomorrow morning. A quick headcount indicates that everyone will fit into your living room, so you invite them all back to your place. They bring the food, set up all the heaters, and the party happens.

This is something you could not have planned for, nor is it something that the people who did plan the party could have expected. Even if they had considered the possibility of the power being out, they would not have known about your house.

Planning systems are not good at situations where you need to improvise. For that, we will consider the Learning school of strategy in the next chapter. In the chapter after that, Systems, we'll look at how you can be prepared for chaotic situations.

10 minute version

In a ten minute strategy, a minute is long enough to sketch out as many as ten steps. If you're doing it in your head, you might want to keep it down to four or five. Don't try to be exhaustive. Think of the key dependencies. Most ten minute strategies need to be executed fairly immediately (otherwise you would take more time to strategise), so the easiest way to sketch is with a flow-chart type. If you are planning a longer term strategy—for example because the situation has just radically changed and you are going into a meeting in ten minutes time in which you will need to present a viable strategy—then you might sketch out a Gantt.

The trick is to stay calm. Work backwards from the goal. Ask yourself 'what has to happen for this to happen?'. You should have a fairly clear idea from the work you've already done.

In our lost children example, the project outcome is that the children are found. For that to happen, someone has to make contact with them. This is a relatively complex project, in the sense that you've got three branching project lines.

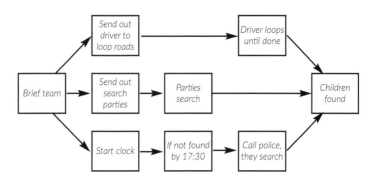

This chart is going to take more than a minute to sketch. The key here is to ignore the 'what if?' side of things and only sketch what you control, thus:

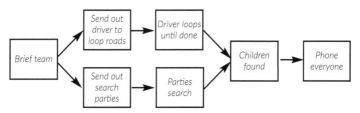

This plan does not represent your full strategy, only the steps you are actively going to take. Simplifying it allows you to think one stage further: how do we call off the search once we've found the children?

This is an important divergence from a Plan-only strategy. For someone trained in project planning, everything must be included. 'If we fail to plan, we plan to fail', as the adage goes. But this requires extending a typical project plan with a decision-tree. Decision trees multiply the complexity of planning, to the point that the tool is no longer useful.

In our hybrid, ten strategy types system, we don't need to plan for everything, just the things that can be reasonably planned.

Two day version

In a two day strategy workshop, moving to Gameplan means a complete change of pace. Members of the group who have until now been quiet and disengaged will come to the front. These are the natural planners, who struggled to grasp why all of the preceding steps were necessary. At the same time, the more conceptual thinkers who enjoyed the preceding steps will become less interested.

For this session, reiterate the Situation, Thinking and Resolve. Restate the 'Results' from the Resolve section, and do so in the SMART format: specific, measurable, agreed, realistic, timed. Check that everyone agrees.

By this point your natural planners have probably already been doodling the plan, if one of them hasn't already gone to the whiteboard and started drawing it out (natural planners are not always good with people and emotions). However, if you want to keep everyone on board, which you will for the following sessions, get them to go through the backwards planning process, starting at the end and working backwards to the initial situation.

Take twenty minutes to do the 'world atlas' level. Some people will want to dive into the detail first. Tell them that you plan to go there in a few minutes.

The easiest way to do this visually is with sticky notes. Write the main programme elements on the notes, and then rearrange them on the white board.

As an example, consider selling your house in England, moving to Brussels, and buying a house there.

Your steps might look something like this:

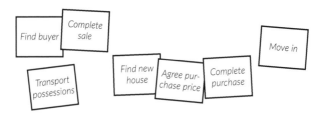

It's obvious that some of these processes must run in sequence: you can't complete your sale until you've found a buyer, you can't move in until you've completed purchase. On the other hand, other sequences can be rearranged. Get the group to decide what the optimal arrangement is.

The result might be something like this:

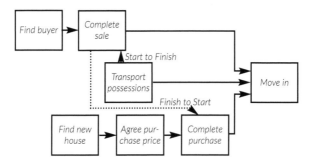

This is probably the arrangement you are looking for. You will notice two constraints. One is that completing the sale requires you to begin to transport your possessions. You can begin transporting before that, but you can't wait longer than that, as the original house is no longer yours. The other is that you must complete the sale on the old house before you complete the purchase of the new house, otherwise you won't have the money to pay for it. In the ideal scenario, you complete the sale of one and the purchase of the other on the same day, and take your possessions straight from one to the other, but this is going to be more complicated when moving from one country to another.

It's now time to go to the next level. This is not yet the 'AtoZ' level. It is more like the Highways Atlas level.

Take forty minutes for this. Space out the sticky notes so that you can put intermediate steps in. Finding a buyer, for example, will require the discreet steps of choosing an estate agent, having them assess the property, and agreeing the sale price. Completing the sale will involve contracting a lawyer and satisfying the purchaser's requirements. Transporting possessions will require booking a haulier, packing, and unpacking. There may be an intermediate step of storing your possessions if there will be a gap between selling one property and buying the next.

You will not have time for the Street Atlas version. This would take you down to the level of purchasing packing materials, obtaining different kinds of legal documents, organising currency transfers, and so on.

Where do you stop? For most projects, you can stop going into further detail at the point you can give someone an unambiguous instruction which falls into their normal job competency. Over-planning by telling people how to do their jobs makes the project less likely to succeed, not more likely.

Three month version

In the three month version, you go down to the Street Atlas level. This means exact planning of resources. You are now no longer concerned simply with the most logical ordering of the elements, the highest level, nor with the implicit steps within those elements, but also with the availability of resources.

Slightly inhumanly, in project planning, people, buildings, money and things are all classed as resources.

If you want to use project planning software, this is the time to invoke it. It should enable you to manage all these resources and 'level', which is to say, extend the length of particular elements to be achievable in available resources. You need to be careful when doing this. If you give your software incomplete information, anything it automates will be nonsensical. If in doubt, avoid automation features and do everything manually.

Returning to our example of a hospital closure, the world atlas level is that there has to be a public consultation, followed by obtaining planning and other permissions, followed by the commissioning of new services, transfer of patients, demolition of the site, construction of the new hospice, and selection of a charity to run it.

At the next level down, these elements can be split out between various project teams. The Communications department will handle the public consultation, and will produce their own plan for it. The Clinical Commissioning department will plan the commissioning of new services and selection of the hospice partner, and other departments take responsibility for their respective areas.

To manage this, focus on milestone events. In a project of this scale, a milestone is typically a Board meeting where a report is received on the previous phase, and a decision is made to go ahead with the next phase. The Board will normally give in-principle permission before the project begins, but then require updates and a decision as each phase ends.

These milestones are the closest project planning gets to branching contingencies. An unexpected Board decision, perhaps following an alarming phase report, means that the planners have to come up with an entirely new plan.

8 Improvements

The Learning or Emergent school of strategy began as a reaction to the Planning school. In its most extreme form, it proposes the Learning Organisation, where the key strategic purpose of a corporate body is to learn. One of the early advocates of this school was Henry Mintzberg. Before analysing all ten schools of strategy, he moved onto Configuration strategy, which we will look at in the final section.

One of the implications of the learning school is that it learns, which is one reason why Mintzberg did not stay with the school he had co-created. While planners tend to dig deeper and deeper into their plans, and therefore fail to understand that even the best plan may be the wrong kind of strategy, learners continually seek to evaluate and question.

Both the Planning and Learning schools of strategy have their flaws, and neither can offer a complete, universal strategy solution.

Strategic question 8: How do we get better as we go?

The most basic aspects of this school are evaluation and adjustment.

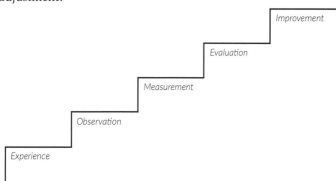

The goal of this section is improvement—and this improvement can go as far as tearing up the entire strategy and starting again, if that's what is needed. This is especially the case in a competitive game with a learning opponent. In such a game, such as football or fencing, you would aim to gain an early advantage with an innovative and unexpected strategy. If everything goes well, this will be a decisive advantage, but there is a real risk that the opponent will identify the strategy too early and execute a counter-strategy. What was intended to give a decisive advantage may actually provide a disadvantage.

The lowest level of learning is **experience**. The tennis player feels that his best serves are being returned unplayably. The fender finds his best attacks are met with devastating ripostes. The football team find themselves outplayed. In some cases, experience is all there is time for, and we have to jump straight to evaluation and improvement.

Where possible, we should at least attempt observation. Somebody not on the field watches and takes notes, and these are used to inform the player or the team at a convenient break. In cricket, which moves at a slower pace, the whole team is observing ball by ball, and wise captains ask for their observations. The difference between observation and experience is that experience focusses on what it's like for us, whereas observation is focussed on the other player or team.

Observation is an improvement on experience, but measurement takes us to a higher level. A hundred years ago this was largely unheard of in sport. Today, every professional team and player has a raft of video-assisted measurements, often supplemented by on-field tools such as speed guns.

Measurement is collated and organised observation, but measurement on its own is insufficient to cause improvement. There must be some form of evaluation. Evaluation applies intelligence to data. This is another way of saying that evaluation contains a dose of opinion, which is in itself a way of saying that you (or someone) applies insight.

Evaluation in itself does not produce improvement. There has been something of an epidemic of (dare we say it?) pointless evaluation over the past thirty years. Sometimes the cost of the evaluation means a substantial cut to the project budget, but the results are only available after it has finished, so there is no opportunity to improve.

At other times, the purpose of the evaluation is no more than to prove value for money against a notional funding target. Evaluation also gets used to 'prove' the value of an under-fire department or external agency.

If you want to improve using evaluation, you need to build it into the strategy from the outset, and design it so that it gives continuous information throughout the programme. There's nothing particularly difficult about doing this, it's just that very few people think of it, and even fewer bother to do it.

To have successful in-project **improvement,** all you need to do is have a way to continually ask the ten strategic questions:

What is our situation?
What's the Big Idea?
Do we dare?
Who is with us?
What are we good at?
What are we doing that's different, and how will we take people with us?
What steps must we take, and in what order?
How do we get better as we go?
How are things arranged?
How will strategy change us?

These questions can be answered in different ways.

You can have **continuously measured information,** such as the speedometer on a car dashboard.

You can have **occasionally measured information,** such as traffic updates on the radio, which you get without interrupting what you're doing, or occasionally measured information such as checking the oil, which requires you to stop the car.

You can have **proxy indicators,** which correlate with something else without directly causing or being caused by it. If you're worried about leaks in the radiator, you can keep a close eye on the temperature gauge, even though this does not specifically measure water levels.

You can have **milestone indicators,** such as road signs. These are different from occasionally measured information, because you can't summon up a road-sign whenever you want it: you have to wait until you get to it.

Often, the best indicators are less formal: they can be 'looking out of the window' indicators, applying your **general awareness** of the situation to the specific questions, or 'ask the passengers' indicators, where the **unstructured observations** of the group tell you things you could not otherwise know. Imagine that your GPS is malfunctioning, and you want to know if you're in Germany or not. You may or may not have passed a sign saying 'welcome to Germany'. However, if one of the passengers has noticed that all the exit signs say 'Ausfahrt' not 'Sortie', which would be France or Belgium, or 'Uitrit', which would be the Netherlands or northern Belgium, then you can be fairly certain that you are in Germany. In principle, you could be in Austria or Switzerland, but **contextual knowledge** should tell you that if that is the case, then you are well and truly lost.

How is this different from just measuring stuff? Directing it with the strategic questions helps you to focus on that which has a strategic result.

This acronym might help you: try to make your measures **Harmless, Useful** and **Efficient** (HUE).

Harmless—try to use measures which don't adversely affect the project. Sending out frequent surveys via a (pseudo)-free online portal may be easy, but your team will get fed up with them fairly quickly, and filling them in takes time out of doing the work.

Useful—for every measure, check that it is answering a strategic question, and that it is producing information you can actually use.

Efficient—look for things which give a relatively high amount of useful information for a comparatively low overhead. Carefully analyse your measures to make sure that you aren't measuring the same thing several different ways, or measuring a sum and its components separately.

Measurement and evaluation should lead to one or more of four things, which make the acronym 'CURE'[17].

Celebrate—use ongoing learning to celebrate the minor victories. This boosts the project, and can help shape culture.

---

17 To 'cure' means to make a sick person well, but also to temper, harden and stabilise metal or leather by a chemical process. 'CURE' is therefore an appropriate acronym, because improvements through evaluation can fix problems and also strengthen the overall project.

Understand—use ongoing learning to discover why some things work and others don't.

Replicate—discover and test what successful elements are unique to the project, and what can be applied elsewhere.

Excel—excellence is not a matter of doing things somewhat better than previously. To be excellent, you need to do what you are doing better than it has been done anywhere, ever. Continuous improvement, rather than inspired one-off improvement, is the faster path to excellence.

10 minute version

In a single minute, you have time to ask and reflect on one question in two parts: what is the single thing that we have to know as we execute this strategy, and by what means will we apply this information to improve what we're doing? You're looking for one measure, and one kind of adjustment.

If you're driving a car, that single measure is looking out of the windscreen at the road ahead, and the adjustment is steering. All other instruments and controls are secondary.

Let's go back to our lost children. What's the single, critical measure? Simply, we need to know if they've been found. Once we know that, we need to be able to recall the teams. Practically speaking, this is a matter of ensuring that each team has a charged mobile phone, that all the numbers have been shared and checked, and that everyone knows to inform the leader and not to fill up the space and empty the batteries with chatter.

Two day version

In this session, we want to construct an improvements 'dash board'. You may have seen these if you work for particular kinds of organisations. However, if we start with the dashboard itself, we're unlikely to get measures that actually help.

Instead, begin by asking the team to imagine they are the end of the project, and it's only been a partial success. Get them to make an imaginative list of:

- Repeated mistakes
- Missed opportunities
- Failures to improve.

Spend about five minutes on this, then re-introduce the Risks from the Resolve session. Let it run for another five minutes. Write the results on sticky notes, and group them.

Now spend ten minutes asking the group to come up with the kinds of information which could have forewarned them. You can rearrange the original sticky notes as you go on.

Don't let them get bogged down in the exact issues they imagined: you are right now trying to get them to think into a particular mindset, rather than solve the imaginary problems.

In the next twenty minutes, draw up six boxes, and ask them to come up with the six key measurements that will do the most to allow you to improve the strategy as it goes on. Remind them of the strategic questions. You don't need to make an explicit link with the first two parts of the session, but let them use what they learned if they want to.

Use the two acronyms, HUE and CURE to steer the session, but do so softly—let the better ideas crowd out the poorer ideas, rather than specifically criticising them.

Keep the conversation going until you have six realistic measures. It can help to draw pictures of different kinds of measuring equipment, such as thermometer, speedometer, fuel gauge, dipstick, and so on.

Finally, ask them to suggest an adjustment mechanism which goes with each of the measurements.

Three month version

Take the work done in the two-day workshop, and analyse the dashboard you've created.

- Are any of the measurements repeating each other?
- Do they give information on all the strategic questions?
- Can they be simplified or reduced?
- Do they create perverse incentives?

Perverse incentives are when the way a measurement is taken or question asked leads people away from desired behaviour. Imagine that you are trying to get school children not to drop litter. If you ask them to measure 'how much litter did you drop today', even without any kind of reward or prize, they will tend to drop more litter, not less. This is a typical perverse incentive. Slightly more subtly, if you ask them how much litter they put into bins, you will find that some of them start putting things into bins which are not actually litter. Fairly soon the bins will overflow, and the litter problem becomes worse. A better measurement is to ask them 'how many areas were entirely litter free when school finished?' This encourages the behaviour you want, and, coincidentally, measures what you want to actually achieve, rather than the action which causes its achievement. Perverse incentives are one of the most common forms of harm caused by ill-considered measurement systems.

Once you're satisfied that these are valuable forms of measurement, investigate how they can be practically achieved. On a sliding scale, the most practical information is that which is already continuously gathered, albeit for another purpose.

In the UK's National Health Service, it was discovered that staff morale, measured annually in a staff attitude survey, correlated closely with time taken off for sickness and other unplanned absences. This is not to suggest that poor morale causes extra sickness, or that sickness contributes to poor morale, but simply that sickness absence is a good proxy indicator. This information was already being gathered, and so could be fed directly into a dashboard without additional work.

At the other end of the sliding scale, anything which has significant lag, requires special effort to gather, and can only be gathered by interrupting a process, is going to be impractical. As well as impacting cost, impractical data collection tends to corrupt the information. If you decide to study satisfaction with the railways by approaching people in a crowded station during rush-hour, then some of the data will show significantly worse satisfaction, because of the annoyance caused by approaching people who are in a hurry, and some of the data will show better satisfaction, once the survey team learn only to approach people who appear to be relaxed and have time on their hands.

Once you are satisfied that you have a set of practical measurements, sketch out three trajectories for each one. The first is the baseline, or expected result if everything goes to plan. For example, if your project is simply a question of getting 3,500 people to sign up for a mailing list, and you have one week to do so, and you can continuously measure how many are signed up, then your trajectory would be a straight line with 500 by the end of Monday, 1,000 by the end of Tuesday, 1,500 by the end of Wednesday, and so on. Second, sketch out the failure trajectory. You don't need to sketch out an 'abject failure' trajectory, but rather a marginal failure. This might be 450 a day, which would give you a final result of 3,150. Finally, sketch out an over-performance trajectory. This is likely to be further from the baseline than the failure trajectory, because most projects are targeted at the minimum success rate. Let's say that the maximum your mailing list can handle is 5,000, so marginal unacceptable overperformance would be 5,500, or 785 a day.

These three scenarios give you your method of evaluation. Without them, you can't tell whether what you're measuring is good and bad.

In a more complex project, you decide to share a quiz on Facebook. Your target is for 10,000 people to have taken the quiz within one week. You have 1,500 Facebook friends, and you recognise that they are going to get annoyed if you keep sharing the same quiz. At the same time, there is no budget for Facebook advertising.

In this case, you are going to share the quiz once, and then rely on its intrinsic shareability to reach those 10,000 people. Because of the network effect, your expected trajectory won't be 143 people a day, but something like 10 on the first day, 100 by the fourth day, 1,000 by the sixth day, and 10,000 by the close of the seventh day. Your expectation is that a proportion of people who take it will share it, and so the number reached grows exponentially rather than linearly.

Let's imagine there's a reason why you can't accept more than 20,000—for example, maybe the quiz site will start charging you if you go over 20,000—but 5,000 would be a fairly serious failure. Your over-success trajectory might look like 12, 144, 1728, 20,000. Your failure trajectory might be 8, 64, 512, 4,000.

Clearly, in this case, the first day's figures don't tell you very much. 8, 10 and 12 are too close to each other to make a judgement. The fourth day figures of 144, 100 and 64 tell you much more. By the time you've hit 1,728, 1,000 or 512, it is too late to do much about it.

After you've drawn your trajectories, consider what levers you can use if under- or over-performing at various points.

This technique, scenario planning, is a powerful method to build in evaluation and action for improvement.

9 Systems

The Design school of strategy is about designing the organisation so that it is perfectly suited to prosper in its environment. By far the most famous method used by the Design School is the SWOT analysis, where you list strengths, weaknesses, opportunities and threats, and then link the strengths to the threats and the opportunities to the weaknesses. The first time you see this done, it looks like magic, and that's effectively what it is: anything which looks like magic, is almost certainly no more than a trick.

As tricks go, it's a good one, and many would-be strategists never get beyond it. Interestingly, though, the Boston Consulting Group (BCG) which created it later abandoned it.

There are several reasons why SWOT is not a form of strategy.

From the point of pure logic, there is absolutely no reason why the strengths should be just right to meet the threats, or the opportunities sufficient to overcome the weaknesses. Imagining that they do is no more than wishful thinking.

Practically speaking, most organisations that take part in such exercises dramatically overstate their strengths and understate their weaknesses, and frequently have little idea of the threats they face, and not much better when it comes to opportunities.

We suggest you don't use SWOT.

But the underlying notion of Design school can usefully supplement what we've already looked at. This late in the process, many of the things it might touch on have been covered by other elements. We are therefore only going to look at what we haven't already dealt with, which is Systems.

Systems, and the Design school generally, are highly useful in chaotic situations. If you look at ambulance services, the police and anti-terrorist units, all of which operate in highly chaotic environments, they are all highly systematic.

Systems are the structural equivalent of tactics. Tactics are things that you do, systems are things that you are. You can call it 'infrastructure' if you prefer.

Your systems include:
- Organisational chart
- Financial systems
- IT and telecommunications systems
- Policies and Procedures
- Governance, constitution, standing orders and by-laws
- Visual identity and brand systems
- Lexicons and vocabularies
- Facilities, fleet and equipment management
- Intelligence, monitoring and newsgathering systems
- Transport, delivery, supply and demand chain systems.

Strategic question 9: How are things arranged?

All the strategy elements we've talked about so far are active. Our theory of strategy—a better way to get from A to B—assumes that there is a B and you want to go there. We'd argue this is intrinsic to the nature of strategy. But there are also things in the category of 'fit and forget', or, at least, 'install and maintain'. In military vocabulary, 'strategic' assets are infrastructural: a tactical weapon knocks out battlefield equipment, a strategic weapon destroys roads and factories. A nation's 'strategic infrastructure' is its power stations, road networks, railways, water supply and communications.

By this point in the strategy, you may have answered all the relevant questions, but it's possible that you haven't, so it is worth looking at the systems your strategy is going to rely on. Consider: the generic term for a school, company, hospital, charity, NGO or government is 'organisation', implying that there has been a deliberate arrangement of the various components so that they function well together.

They do not all live up to the name. Some organisations are more of a collection than a system. Random tasks make their way across a bleak landscape of partially installed equipment. This is common when an organisation has a gold mine of some kind: a monopoly of a scarce resource which ensures income and status, and disguises dysfunction.

At the national level, several oil-rich states were in this position before the sudden and unexpected drop in the price of oil in the early 2010s. Government corruption, massive unemployment, systemic incompatibilities and a lack of overall direction were masked by the constant flow of cash into the economy. When the oil price fell, these states one by one tumbled into collapse or chaos.

You will seldom have time to perform a comprehensive review of the entire organisation, and comprehensive reviews are rarely successful: they attract tooo much attention, so vested interests have time to repackage what they are doing so that the review does little more than concentrate power in the hands of the already powerful.

However, even in rapid strategy, you can usually spot the assets you are going to rely on most heavily, and identify whether they are working for you or against you. Generally speaking, they will be arranged around the status quo, which is to say that they will, at best, be incompletely aligned with what you want to do.

In our experience, organisations tend to be either ring doughnuts, or layer cakes. The doughnut is organised around a previous powerful, strategic idea, but that idea is now gone, leaving a hole in the middle. The layer cake is made of up historic layers of partial reorganisations. Each new layer protects the layers below, and makes it harder to change them.

If you are new to an organisation, you should take the time to understand it: although unusual, it is possible that your organisation has been well constructed and is both efficient and effective. It's also possible that the organisation is entirely dysfunctional, without any coordination between the differing parts.

We are here talking about the extent to which the organisation is built to suit its environment, not its particular shape, which we will look at in the final section. Different environments call for different shapes: an underwater base at some depth is going to look very different from a space station. A castle built to withstand attacks is going to be a fundamentally different form from a garden centre.

When an organisation is well-organised, it has the following characteristics:

Effectiveness—it is able to fulfil its function consistently at an appropriate scale and speed.

Efficiency—it yields a high return on the resources deployed, with a low level of wastage.

Elegance—it is apparent in many places that thought has gone into the way things are done.

Emulation—the organisation in some way reflects the environment it exists in.

Ease of navigation—it is a simple matter to find where to go for particular functions.

The well designed organisation looks exactly as you would expect—it has been designed for its job rather than repurposed.

There's a simple hierarchy to consider when you want to change the design. Essentially, seek to achieve the changes you need with the least disruption, by changing that which it more temporary in preference to that which is more permanent.

In most organisations, changing how and what you communicate is the least disruptive change. Therefore, communicate first, and communicate widely.

If your organisation has deliberate, published policies, protocols or procedures, the next level is typically to modify or update them.

Changing the leadership of the organisation will often, though not always, be the next least-disruptive change.

Reallocation of budgets comes after that. In most organisations this is painful, but less painful than the subsequent layers.

Changing the organisational chart, job structure or hierarchy is more painful. Essentially, any major change in job structure which is going to survive less than two years is wasted effort.

Heavy or widely deployed equipment, such as a computer network, is typically harder to redesign than staff structures.

Partnerships, including supply chain and demand chain, are almost the last thing you should consider changing.

Finally, facilities are the most permanent and enduring aspect of most organisations. Even minor rebuilding work can cause problems. If you wish to close a wing, or a building, or manage a relocation, then your strategy will be primarily about that.

1O minute version

In one minute, you have time to ask yourself: is there an aspect of communication, policy, leadership, budgets, job structure, equipment, partnerships of facilities which is obviously in the way? You could look for the following:

Choke points—under-resourced units which slow everything down. They either need to be better resourced or bypassed.

Autonomous gatekeepers—individuals or committees that must give their approval to a decision already made at a more appropriate place.

Loose cannons—individuals or units which are able to and choose to act outside of the main strategy.

Gold-platers—individuals or units which add additional requirements onto the organisation's strategy.

If you don't see any of these, don't worry: we are just looking for obvious problems.

If the situation which has caused you to need a strategy has something to do with a failure of organisation or infrastructure, there are two more things to look for straight away:

Dead circuits—some previously functioning system has failed. This might be because a piece of equipment or physical infrastructure has failed, or perhaps because a person has gone off sick, or changed job.

Infinite loops and wild readings—a flaw in the design of your system means that the same form is being passed round again and again, or someone is being sent from person to person without ever getting closer to resolution, or the system is oscillating from one thing to another.

Dead circuits and infinite loops/wild readings are more likely in highly organised, automated organisations. They can arise because something has recently gone wrong, or because an issue has arisen that has never been tested before. More worrying, the symptom which has triggered your strategy may be just the first time it came to your attention.

If there are no obvious problems, ask yourself: what channel am I most going to rely on to execute this strategy? Is this clear? If not, how do I clear it?

In our missing children example, the channel we are going to rely on, as noted in the previous section, is mobile phones. For this channel to work, we need three things: functioning mobile phones on a functioning network, knowledge of each other's numbers, and a commitment by the teams to check their mobiles and to report in. This is typically the kind of level at which a ten minute strategy is going to operate. There may be some very serious problems with organisation and infrastructure, but these are for another day.

Two day version

In the two day version, we are going to take an hour to map out our key processes. Most organisations have hundreds of processes, and some organisations, such as England's National Health Service (NHS) with 1.2 million employees, have thousands. However, even in the largest organisations, there will usually just be three or four key processes.

For the NHS, the key processes are these:

1 How money gets from the government to health providers to pay the costs that patients incur.

2 How patients are referred for the correct treatment from their family doctor to whichever service they need.

3 How patient safety and clinical effectiveness are assured so that patients get the right treatment at the right time from the right person in the right place.

4 How infrastructure is maintained so that the health service is available when people need it.

In introducing this session (unless your team is working in the NHS) you might begin with this example, or a similar example from another Very Large, Very Complex Organisation (vlvco) that nonetheless can be understood in a few main processes.

Giving this, or another example of a VLVCO should take about five minutes.

In the next fifteen minutes, ask them to identify your organisation's key processes. It may help to ask "what do we actually do?" but don't push this too hard: sometimes the processes demonstrate that what your organisation does isn't what it thinks it does.

Now, take a deep breath: ask 'what typically goes wrong with these processes'? You have forty minutes left in the session, and you could easily use the whole time scribbling on the white board, flip chart or sticky notes as people pour out their grief about things going wrong. You'll need to stop the conversation after twenty minutes, though, because, much as it is therapeutic, identifying these things will only allow you to fix the 'how': it won't touch the 'why' or the 'what'.

For the final twenty minutes, ask people to consider if there are any major systems which are missing, redundant, or misaligned. In other words, are the systems which are in place the right ones for the task you have?

It is all too easy to expend effort in improving the wrong systems. In one hospital we looked at, staff were hand-copying paper forms from an emergency department intake when a patient was transferred to a ward. The system could have been improved by having just one form that didn't need to be copied. However, an altogether better system would have been to enter the patient details onto computer at the point of arrival, and link them to the patient's electronic health record.

As they discuss this, try to steer them away from anything which involves adopting another infrastructure which they've seen at work somewhere else. Otherwise you get into something similar to the website entropy cycle, where someone says "our website is not as good as the one down the road". Someone replies by saying that the other website uses Drupal, or WordPress, or Concrete5, or any other system other than the one you're currently using. A project is created to put the website onto that system. This takes a year. At the end of it, not enough time has been allocated to populate it with content, so the content is largely copied from the existing website. The result is that the website is no better (and is now suffering from the different set of problems inherited from the new architecture), and the cycle begins again.

Three month version

Assuming you've identified the key processes, their problems, and the missing or misaligned processes in your two-day session, you now have a week to investigate. Ask for a meeting with the person in charge of each process, and get them to explain to you how it really works, and how they would change it if they could. Sometimes, these people will have wanted to change it for years, but are being held back by perceived resistance from other departments. At the end of the meeting, ask if you can talk to a front-line worker who is involved with the process. In a hospital, talking to the porters will often give you far more information than any of the directors ever knew. As we've seen elsewhere, people at the low-end of an organisation's pay-hierarchy often already have answers to its pressing problems, but are not given a voice on strategic issues.

It's our experience that a week spent investigating intractable problems of organisation generally yields substantial fruit, even when the strategy that led to it is never pursued. To some extent, there's a danger that an under-pressure chief-executive will accept 'easy' improvements in systems and structures which are relatively cheap and extremely uncontroversial, while dodging the more serious strategic issues of direction and route. Removing obstructions is popular, and will be applauded, but it will not solve the fundamental problem unless those things were the fundamental problem. Sometimes that is enough. Usually it is only enough to provide breathing room to tackle the real problems.

If you're in a situation that the Board, or whoever you report to, seems likely to accept your package of efficiency improvements but ignore your overall strategy, then it may be worth presenting it in these terms: right now, we are in a situation we can't get out of, with no room to manoeuvre. Here is a package of measures which will give us that room, but the relief will be short-lived: unless we tackle the strategic problems, we are only delaying the inevitable.

10 Transformation

After the Emergent school, but before writing Strategy Safari, Henry Mintzberg created the Configuration school, which he also referred to as the Transformation school. Fundamentally, he suggests that organisations have a particular shape, which might come from any number of causes, but this is not necessarily the right shape for what the organisation needs to be. Transformation strategy, then, is about changing an organisation from one shape into another.

If this sounds a little like the Design school, you're not far wrong: the Design school is looking for an organisation which has been designed to face its environment. Mintzberg's Configuration school doesn't assume that the organisation has been designed at all, but proposes that shape has a fundamental impact on its effectiveness. From a configuration point of view, changing that shape is what strategy is all about.

If this sounds somewhat confusing, you should know that Mintzberg's book on the subject is several hundred pages long.

But that doesn't mean we should ignore it. In fact, the ideas behind it are the culmination of our whole process.

Executing a strategy changes the organisation. This cannot be avoided, and it doesn't need to be. In the words of one recent US President: never waste a good crisis. Even if the shape of the organisation was right for the previous situation, it almost certainly isn't right for the situation which will follow successful completion of the strategy.

Considering this when putting the strategy together means that you can deliberately steer the organisation in the right direction, rather than letting unexpected changes rule. Many organisations have successfully navigated a crisis, re-invented themselves, moved into a period of success, and then collapsed because of the inevitable tensions in their new shape.

You might be inclined to say that 'it is better to have loved and lost than not have loved at all', and an organisation that has significant success for a while is preferable to one which remains for ever in dismal mediocrity. However, you are crediting such an organisation with the same level of intelligence as yeast, which reproduces uncontrollably up to the point at which it is killed by the alcohol it produces.

Strategic question 10: How will strategy change us?

Mintzberg has six configuration diagrams representing different kinds of organisations. We've found these diagrams to be less successful than the underlying idea, so we're not going to cover them here. You can find them in Strategy Safari if you want them, and in much greater detail in 'The Strategy Process'[18].

Rather than trying to fit your organisation to one of Mintzberg's types, try sketching out how it looks to you. It doesn't actually matter how you sketch it.

18 The Strategy Process - European Edition (Revised),:Mintzberg, Henry, James Brian Quinn, and Sumantra Ghoshal, Prentice Hall, 1998.

In one organisation, participants in a focus group decided that it was like a village high street, where different functions took place in different buildings without necessarily much co-ordination between them, but with the potential for a high degree of social interaction in the public space. We redesigned the organisation on this basis, and saw morale, productivity and effectiveness soar.

It doesn't actually matter whether the sketch makes sense to anyone else, as long as it makes sense to the people in the organisation.

The only thing I would counsel against is going for an easy analogy, such as 'we're one big happy family', or 'we're a team'. These ideas have already been exploited to death, and you're unlikely to gain new insights from them.

Let's look at a few examples, and how they might be applied.

One way of looking at an organisation is to say it's like a tent. A tent is portable, allows the breeze through, which is nice in summer, and allows you to hear what's going on around you, which is nice at a festival. But it's not very secure: even if you padlocked the front, someone could just take a knife and open it up.

Another way is to say an organisation is like a plant, bringing in resources from the roots, transforming them by photosynthesis, expelling oxygen to the benefit of those around and growing more stable and beautiful.

Or you could say that the organisation is like an ant hill, with each worker behaving in pre-defined patterns, which may appear uncoordinated, but which produce an effective and sustainable result with its own beauty and symmetry.

Now, the question is, if the strategy is successfully fulfilled, what could we become? Supposing you could transmogrify from a tent into a battle-ship, or from a plant into a dragon?

What would be the ideal kind of organisation if your strategy is successfully completed?

The shape of Britain between 1950 and 2000 was in a large measure defined by the NHS. It was the one institution that everybody engaged with, and it cared for them from the cradle to the grave. The NHS did not come about by wishful thinking. It was a direct product of the Second World War. People voted for it because they were promised 'a land fit for heroes'. The country could afford it because it had learned to live within its means during the war years. It was high in public priorities, because war had brought about an unusual amount of health emergencies. It was technically feasible, because the discovery of penicillin meant that thousands of previously fatal conditions could be successfully treated, and techniques of patient care had taken a leap forward, as they often does in wartime.

It's hard to second-guess the past (or all too easy, put another way), but it seems unlikely that without the successful execution of the wartime strategy, the NHS would ever have happened. Certainly it would not have happened if Britain had lost the war, but, even if the war had never happened, or had reached a negotiated peace in its early days, it is hard to imagine the conditions of the 1930s producing it. More likely, available money would have gone into stabilising the economy and shoring up the banks, so that the economic crisis of 1928 could never occur again.

Very large strategies produce the opportunities for very large changes in configuration. Commensurately, smaller strategies allow smaller, though still significant, changes.

The most basic output of any successful strategy is a belief within the organisation that 'strategy works'. A reactive organisation can become pro-active, and an over-aggressive organisation can learn to think first and act afterwards.

Consider a fencer in en garde position. Any coach can tell you that they should have their weight evenly distributed across both feet, but most fencers don't do that. Overly-aggressive fencers tend to lean forwards, with their weight on the front feet. Overly-defensive fencers lean back. In reality both are counter-productive: a fencer leaning forward loses mobility to attack, and a fencer leaning backward loses mobility to retreat. With help from the coach, most fencers can correct this in practice sessions, but it is the ones who discover correct balance during a fight—especially a competition fight which means a lot to them—that tend to flourish. Abilities won during the heat of conflict are more precious and become ingrained more deeply.

So it is with strategy: an organisation that learns to think and act, instead of just think (bias toward inaction) or just act (bias toward aggression), and as a result digs its way out of an otherwise intractable situation will take the lessons to heart, as long as they are subsequently spelled out.

Successful strategy is always at risk of hostile renarration. After a highly successful (and, eventually, internationally published) campaign that ran for three years, our programme was evaluated by another organisation that wished to promote its own services and strategic model—a model fundamentally at odds with ours. Unsurprisingly, since they were measuring us against adherence to their model, they ruled the programme as substandard. But they were left with the question: if the strategy was wrong, why were the results right? Their conclusion was that there must have been some additional, undisclosed outside factor. The programme reached its conclusion, but was not renewed. Afterwards, results slumped to their previous unacceptable level.[19]

---

19 To finish the story, although that campaign finished, we were engaged by other parts of the organisation for much larger and more urgent campaigns, which were evaluated by genuinely independent external bodies, and performed very well. The competitor organisation was disbanded.

This is not unusual: most strategies have their advocates and their detractors, and if the detractors get to write the final report, you can expect any organisational learning or transformation will be lost.

1O minute version

In a single minute, you have time to think: 'what are the outcomes of the strategy going to be?' This includes the failure outcomes as well as the success outcomes. Both success and failure offer possibilities to transform the organisation, if you see the end from the beginning. However, if you wait to the end, you will have missed the opportunity. You must therefore decide how to build the final transformation in right at the start.

Think back to the lost children scenario:

"You have just taken over as the national director of a youth organisation at your annual team retreat in Luxembourg."

In this particular case, you are pushed into a formative moment, the like of which you could not have generated even if you had planned it. Whether the strategy succeeds or fails, it will mark the organisation for ever.

It's possible that, recognising this is a defining moment, you will want to choose to play it safe and call the police straight away, reasoning that the damage done by failure outweighs any good that might come from success. This 'strategy not to have a strategy' is something we've often seen. However, psychologically, especially for the parents, this is worse than outright failure. For ever, your leadership will be characterised by the tag 'he didn't even try'.

Another option which is unproductive, though not to the same extent, is to wait and see what the outcome is, and then try to narrate it. Essentially, you are then acting as no more than a commentator on your own adventure—and more authoritative-sounding commentators may tell the story a very different way.

Your team can see the situation just as well as you can. They recognise there are two possible outcomes, one of which is deeply painful. What you say to keep them motivated during the crisis will be remembered far more than any commentary you try to attach to it afterwards.

Some of the ways you can bring about transformation with only a minute to plan are:

Who you ask to take a lead. You can introduce new leaders, or raise the perceived importance of particular roles.

What your strategic idea is. A radically creative strategy, if successful, will empower creative strategists. An execution of tried-and-tested plans will empower the planners.

When you choose to act. For some strategies, going straight away is the right approach. In others, holding your nerve until the last moment is the key. In most cases, there will be a range of choices.

Where you choose to deploy your resources. This could be a physical where, but it can also be where in the organisation's structure. If you want to see front-line staff play more of a role in the future, then engage them early in the strategy.

How you behave during implementation. People look to the leader for a model. You may be in despair, in which case you may need to find help from another source.

The reasons you give for why you are doing what you do. People will see quickly where your values lie.

Two day version

The two day version allows for a rather more deliberate approach. Take twenty minutes to ask people to describe what the organisation is like now. Encourage far-fetched comparisons, so long as the people who propose them are willing to explain. Find the one which most people think is the most reasonable.

In the second twenty minutes, ask them to think what the ideal shape of the organisation will be after the strategy is fully executed. Give them the freedom to think big. Merger with one of the allies is a possibility, or spinning off a functional unit into a separate organisation. For some kinds of strategy, reconfiguration is more or less compulsory, so you may already have answered the key questions. For others, long-term changes can flow from short-term solutions.

In the final twenty minutes, which will be the final creative section of the strategy process, ask them to decide how they can build movement toward the new, better configuration into the flow of the strategy. This can turn into a rather fuzzy brainstorm, so go back over the answers to the ten strategic questions. For each one, ask them to offer one bad solution and one good solution, so you end up with a list of ten 'Instead of doing A, we will do B'.

Three month version

As you bring the strategy formation process to a close, in the final week visit the parts of the organisation and its allies that you want to see changed as the renewed organisation takes shape. Ask them to tell you their hopes, ambitions and fears, and use these to develop the new shape, while also weaving into the conversation your own ambition for this new shape. Your initial idea is almost certainly not the best possible idea: a shape which has been drawn up by consensus, taking account of the expertise people already have will be substantially better than the one you drew up with a small group, even though that small group may have determined the overall direction.

Becoming a strategist

To become the ten minute strategist that we talked about in this book, it will take a lot more than ten minutes. You need to practise over and over again. Almost any problem, situation or opportunity presents a chance to try it.

Situation	What is our situation?
Thinking	What's the Big Idea?
Resolve	Do we dare?
Allies	Who is with us?
Tactics	What are we good at?
Embedding	What are we doing that's different, and how will we take people with us?
Gameplan	What steps must we take, and in what order?
Improvements	How do we get better as we go?
Systems	How are things arranged?
Transformation	How will strategy change us?

In doing so, resist the temptation to go deep too early. Start off with the ten minute version. You may go on to spend much longer on particular aspects of a strategy, or on all of it, but getting the rhythm of creating a complete strategy rapidly is important.

We said at the beginning that the STRATEGIST process is iterative. Once you've got to the end, you will want to change some things earlier on, and these may have knock-on effects. This is one reason why you want to get the overall shape down in one go: it is all too easy to spend hours on a particular aspect, only to discover that it is invalidated by later thinking.

Knowing all of this is the beginning. To become a strategist, you need to practice strategy. Find opportunities. Take part in competitive sport. Watch the news and work out how you would tackle a particular situation. Sketch out strategies on the back of a paper napkin while you wait in Starbucks for a friend.

Explaining the strategy

Forming the strategy and explaining it are two completely different things. If you give too much detail, people will either think you are patronising them, or else they will get lost.

Let's imagine you've bought an automatic transmission car for the first time, and you notice that it doesn't accelerate the way your old manual transmission car did. So you ask the garage "how do I get more acceleration?" The answer you want to hear is "jam your foot hard down on the accelerator. The engine will then know to go down a gear and switch on any other little tricks it has." The garage mechanic could equally well say: "the car is controlled by an electronic control unit, known as an ECU. This continually monitors the engine and tunes it for an optimum balance of performance and economy. This restricts flow of fuel to the engine, and keeps the injection, turbo-charger and other performance features in high economy mode, while keeping you in the highest possible gear for your speed. However, there is a sensor in the accelerator pedal that, when fully depressed, informs the ECU that you now wish to go into performance mode. The ECU then drops the gears to a more aggressive ratio, changes the mode on the turbo-charger and injection, and maximises flow of fuel to the engine. This gives you a performance lift at the expense of fuel economy."

This is the wrong answer. If you are interested in cars and know lots about them, you almost certainly already know all this, and just want to know how to engage performance mode on this car. If you are only interested in faster acceleration, it's too much information.

However, it's not the worst possible answer. The mechanic could begin by explaining to you how the internal combustion engine works.

Talking about strategy is similar. When people ask 'what's our strategy?', they don't want to go through the whole process with you. They want the one big idea.

This big idea may be the strategic idea from the Thinking section, but it may also be a three point plan, or opening negotiations with allies, or changing the shape of the organisation.

With the lost children, the answer people need to hear is the gameplan: "we're going to send out search parties through the forest, while a driver and a spotter go round the road loop so they can find the boys if they emerge from the forest. We'll do this for two hours. If we haven't found them by then, we'll call the police."

With closing the hospital, the answer is "our job is to work for the best interests of the patients. We'll listen to what local people have to say, listen to doctors, and look at affordability, but ultimately it comes down to patient safety, clinical effectiveness, and patient experience." This answer is essentially stating the Resolve section.

If you're setting long-term strategy for health across an entire region, the answer might be "best health for everyone—we want to help each person to have the best health they can, within the strictures of what is best for everyone". This is the Big Idea from the Thinking section.

How do you choose what to say? If you know that the person you're talking to is from a particular strategic background, then you obviously need to couch it in language they will accept, otherwise they will simply say 'that's not a strategy'.

The fundamental thing to remember is what we said right at the beginning:

"If you reach a fork in the road, and you don't know whether your strategy says go left or right, then you don't have a strategy."

The way you explain your strategy needs to be something which is memorable and actionable. For the lost children, everyone knows to keep searching until 17:30, or until they hear the children are found, and then return to base. For the hospital closure, the Board, when it comes to making a decision, needs to look back and say "Patient Safety, Clinical Effectiveness, Patient Experience—what's the best choice to achieve these things?" For the health service across a region, any doctor, nurse, physiotherapist or hospital porter has to be able to say: "What is 'best health for everyone' in this situation? What's best for this patient, and will this be so expensive that it starts to damage care for others?"

In the film the Seven Samurai, which we discussed on page 36, the big idea is 'hire Samurai', but all of the other aspects of the STRATEGIST framework come into play.

Situation—strategy begins with correctly assessing the situation. Without this, nothing else would have happened.

Thinking—the big idea is 'hire Samurai'.

Resolve—the villagers send out some of their number to recruit Samurai, and decide what they are willing to pay to recruit them.

Allies—they find initially one Samurai, who recruits the other six.

Tactics—the Samurai fortify the village and teach the villagers how to use weapons.

Embedding—the villagers learn that hiring Samurai is not enough, they must also be willing to fight.

Gameplan—the Samurai realise that they will not be able to withstand an attack from all the bandits, so they launch their own pre-emptive attack, substantially weakening the bandits, though also incurring losses.

Improvements—the plans develop when the Samurai discover that the villagers have a large supply of armour and weapons looted from Samurai battles, which they have been keeping secret.

Systems—an infrastructure of lookouts and fortifications is created.

Transformation—at the end of the story, with just two Samurai surviving, the villagers are now in a position to fight for themselves, should the need arise again.

If asked to give a one sentence summary of the film, you could use almost any of these, plus the title, to say what the film was about. You could also expand substantially on any of these vignettes.

This particular film is perhaps a special case: it is fundamentally about strategy, which was a subject close to the hearts of the Samurai caste in Japanese society. If you were to summarise Star Wars in strategic terms, you would probably go with the big idea, which is 'Use the Force, Luke', and say that everything else comes together because of it. Oceans 11, both in the original and the remade version, is a film about a plan, where most of the fun is in concealing the plan from the viewers.

Ultimately, a strategy is a narrative about the future. If you can tell the story interestingly in a couple of sentences, then people will buy into it. If you can't, then they won't.

You might like to consider this simple structure:

Our strategy is [whatever you've decided is the best way to express it succinctly].

Right now, we're *here* [state the situation], but we need to get *there* [state the destination]. To do that, we need to do *this* [state the Big Idea].

What we have to do now is decide whether we're really going to go for it. It will mean *these* [the results, resources, risks, and resistance], but success will mean *this* [the rewards].

These [state the allies] will probably back us, but *those* [state the enemies] will not be happy, so we'll need to negotiate.

Some of the methods we're going to use include… [the tactics].

That's going to mean a change for our organisation, but we think we can show people why it's necessary, and that it's the right thing to do. [This is the embedding].

Simply put, our plan is… [give the three point version of the plan].

Not everything is going to go to plan, so we'll be learning and improving as we go. [Improvements].

There's a couple of blocked channels [state the Systems issues] which have been troubling us for some time. Unblocking them will give us the room to manoeuvre, at least for a while.

All this is going to change us. Right now we're like *this* [current configuration], but we're going to end up looking more like *that* [final configuration].

If asked to go into more detail, you can give a short paragraph on each of these.

To state the strategy in its simple form should take about fifteen seconds, no more. Doing the more explicit version, as we've just looked at, should take from one to three minutes. If it's taking more than three minutes, you've gone into too much detail.

Executing strategy

Except in draughts, chess, sudoku, and a few simple board games, executing strategy is principally about working with people. If everything else that has come before in this book has been obvious and second nature to you, then this may be the point at which you say "I'm not a people person—I can't do it."

You may be extreme 'I' on the Myers-Briggs index, and you may be scoring 25+ on the autism scale, but anybody who is not in a secure clinical unit can learn to work with people. Actually, the extreme extroverts that you may have come across—the ones who always seem to have a party hanging around them—have their own problems as well. They are attractive to other extroverts, but to the more reserved they just seem shallow and over-enthusiastic.

If you're not a 'people person', but recognise that you need to work with people, you need only remember (and apply) these four simple principles.

First, *try always to see things through the other person's eyes*. Everyone makes sense to themselves. You may believe that their behaviour, views and ideals are utterly irrational, but to them it makes perfect sense.

Second, *sweeten everything you do with the politeness patterns of the culture you're in*. This is where you can get ahead of the extroverts, who assume that every culture is the same as theirs. If you're a more reflective person, use this to learn what makes things polite. This goes for email and phone conversations as well as face to face.

Third, *learn to separate your message from your outcome*. You might think that it is most efficient to state what you want, but that isn't how people work. Thinking of things from their perspective, your message is what you think they will find inspiring and persuasive.

Fourth, *learn to respect their time, space and physical needs*. Accurately assessing and meeting these needs is the heart of what leadership is about. People will not care about how much you know, until they know how much you care.

As a bonus fifth point, *learn to ask*. If someone turns up for a meeting at the right time, in the right place, but looks completely disengaged, it's ok to ask if they're ok. They may have had unexpected bad news, they may be unwell, they may not have slept that night, they may be cross with you for some unrelated reason. People won't always tell you what the problem is, but they usually appreciate you asking.

On the other hand, if all that was second nature to you, it is worth reflecting on how you come across to introverts and people with generally limited social skills (which is not all introverts, or just introverts). Your easy charisma and way with words may strike them as lightweight, flighty, untrustworthy and glib. This can be just as much a barrier to effectively delivering a strategy.

Whatever your people skills, being able to motivate, lead and direct a team will be crucial.

But that is the topic for another book.

Before we finish, just two more things: yes, we did build the hospice and, yes, we did find the missing boys.

Mnemonics

CLEVER, Creative, Loose-ended, Emergent, Valuable, Easy, Repeatable, a method for setting goals.

CPM, Critical Path Management, a method for managing projects

CSV, Comma Separated Values, a text file format for data

CURE, Celebrate, Understand, Replicate, Excel: uses of evaluation for improvement

HUE, Harmless, Useful, Efficient, a test for types of measurment

PERT, Programme Evaluation and Review Technique, a formal method for project management

PESTLES, Political, Economic, Social, Technical, Legal, Ecological, Spiritual, a mnemonic for analysing situations

SMART, Specific, Measurable, Achievable, Realistic, Timed, a method for formatting goals within the Planning school of strategy

STRATEGIST, Situation, Thinking, Resolve, Allies, Tactics, Embedding, Gameplan, Improvements, Systems, Transformation: what this book is about, a ten step method of comprehensive strategy construction

SWOT, Strengths, Weaknesses, Opportunities, Threats, a situational analysis model once favoured within the Design school of strategy

VLVCO, Very Large, Very Complex Organisations, such as the UK's National Health Service (NHS).

Index

33474582R00079

Printed in Great Britain
by Amazon